GW00599486

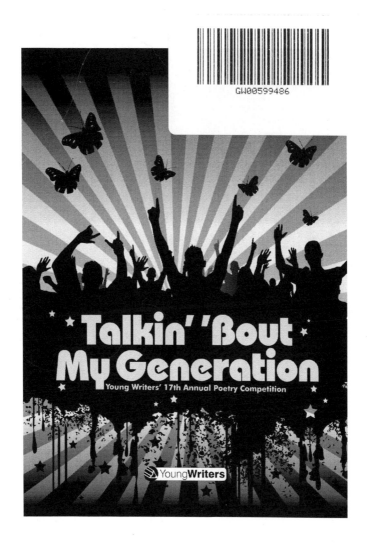

Talkin' 'Bout My Generation

Young Writers' 17th Annual Poetry Competition

YoungWriters

Sussex & Surrey

Edited by Donna Samworth

 Young **Writers**

First published in Great Britain in 2008 by:
Young Writers
Remus House
Coltsfoot Drive
Peterborough
PE2 9JX
Telephone: 01733 890066
Website: www.youngwriters.co.uk

All Rights Reserved

© Copyright Contributors 2007

SB ISBN 978-1 84431 484 3

Foreword

This year, the Young Writers' *Talkin' 'Bout My Generation* competition proudly presents a showcase of the best poetic talent selected from thousands of up-and-coming writers nationwide.

Young Writers was established in 1991 to promote the reading and writing of poetry within schools and to the young of today. Our books nurture and inspire confidence in the ability of young writers and provide a snapshot of poems written in schools and at home by budding poets of the future.

The thought, effort, imagination and hard work put into each poem impressed us all and the task of selecting poems was a difficult but nevertheless enjoyable experience.

We hope you are as pleased as we are with the final selection and that you and your family continue to be entertained with *Talkin' 'Bout My Generation Sussex & Surrey* for many years to come.

Contents

Eleanor Friston (11)   25
Josiah Odimah-Manson (11)   25
Ilar Bristo (11)   26
Sammy Neal   26
Scott Dance (11)   27
Charlotte Ayley-Poulter (11)   27
George Ackerman (12)   28
Amy Cotton (11)   28
Charlotte White (12)   29
Luke Adam Charlton (11)   29
Emily Hughes (11)   30
Laura Evans (11)   30
Bradley Smith (11)   31
Brooke Doughorty (11)   31
Samuel Cates (11)   32
Charlie Lyon (11)   32
Aaron Riches (12)   33

Glyn Technology School, Epsom
Denver Miller (13)   33
Ata Chaudhry (11)   34
James Stone (11)   35
Ekrem Yuksel Demeni (11)   36
Alex Malyon (11)   37
Cayden Nel (13)   38
Dimitri Constantinou (12)   39

Gordon's School, Woking
Nicky Britton-Williams (13)   40
Amira Arasteh (13)   41

Hazelwick School, Crawley
James Watson (11)   42
Jess Grist (11)   42
Jade Coulstock (11)   43
Sophie Tubb (11)   43
Josh Wells (11)   44
Adesh Ajmani (11)   44
Viqas Hussain (15)   45
Nicola Stevens (11)   45
Alanna Hyatt (11)   46

St Andrew's CE High School, Croydon

St Richard's Catholic College, Bexhill-on-Sea

St Teresa's School, Dorking

Seaford College, Petworth

Surbiton High School, Kingston upon Thames

Brodie Prowse (112)	154
Grace Miller (11)	154
Tamara Mulley (11)	155
Bethan Baxter (12)	155
Antonia Adams (12)	156
Josie Chamberlain (12)	156
Grace Martin (13)	157
Hannah Wood (11)	157
Amanda Stafford (13)	158
Zoe Hill (13)	159
Annabel Harris (13)	160
Jessica Heyward-Chaplin (12)	161
Fenella Boulter (12)	1632
Lucy Purslow (13)	163
Ravleen Kaur (13)	1654
Emma Mills (11)	165
Brittany Borkan (12)	166
Kathryn Fletcher (12)	166
Holly Harrison (14)	167
Beth Pollington (11)	167
Viki James (13)	168
Atifa Jiwa (13)	169
Cecilia Seo (14)	170
Sophie Kiedaisch (12)	171
Rosie Morris (13)	172
Amber Fraser (11)	172
Abigail Spence (11)	172
Alexandra Hartley (11)	173
Laura Jones (11)	173
Becky Ridpath (11)	173
Kate Hosker (15)	174
Molly Shingler (12)	175
Isabelle Bettany (11)	176
Abigail Marrow (12)	176
Caroline Croft (14)	177
Amani Patel (13)	177
Rosie Frost (13)	178
Ana Grgurinovic (13)	179
Rosie Jones (12)	180

Tolworth School for Girls, Surbiton

Rebecca Desmond & Charlotte Keenan (9)	180
Eliza Forshaw (17)	181
Soyoung Lee (14)	182
Cara Hitt (13)	182
Nadia Butt (13)	183
Bonita Brincat (14)	183

Varndean School, Brighton

Connie Noble (11)	184
Amber Pearce (11)	184
Anoushka Clayton-Walshe (11)	185
Declan O'Reilly (11)	185
Megan Atkins (11)	186
Connor Macey (12)	187
Lauren Kane-Simmons (12)	188
Ruby Anderson-Hawkins (11)	188
Jack Woodhouse (11)	189
Liam Bailey (11)	189
Jake Crunden (11)	190
Sujan Thapa (13)	190
Alex Bradley (11)	191
Eleanor Sopp (11)	191
Tallulah Pepperell (11)	192
Jack Lawrence (11)	192
Ned Wall (12)	193
Matt Morrish (11)	193
Navan Jarnail Singh Johal (11)	194
Olivia Sewell (11)	194
Raya Alkhayal (11) & Alyce Orford (12)	195
Louise Flowers (11)	195
Jordan Crunden (11)	196
Ian Penny (11)	196
Ciara Smith (11)	196

Wallington High School for Girls, Wallington

Shona Kumar (13	197
Hannah Oram (13)	198
Shaili Desai (13)	199
Xanthe Francis (12)	199
Thayaruby Uthayakumaranathan (12)	200

The Poems

Whirling Respect

A teenage girl,
She now looks so sad,
She had to offer her helping hand,
A mouth of abuse she got in return,
Insider her anger felt like Hell's hot burn.

Prior to that, a different girl,
Offered a helping hand,
And when the lady gave gracious thanks,
The girl ran off with her notes from the banks.

But you have to realise,
You have to learn,
That more of us are like the girl who burned,
We understand,
We know the fact,
That offered help, may punch a pact,
But please listen,
Please open your ears,
Do not treat us with cowardice and fears,
Treat us with the respect that we deserve,
And our respect then shall be served.

Hannah O'Connor (14)

Bad Habits

Everyone's got bad habits,
But it's a real shame,
Whenever anything goes wrong,
Teenagers are to blame.

People say we're lazy,
People say we're crap,
That's why I want to tell you,
'Bout the teenager rap.

OK, there are some hoodies,
Who skulk around the street,
Terrorising everybody,
That they meet.

But if I'm hanging on a corner,
Laughing with my mate,
Crossing to avoid us?
Makes me well irate!

People say we're lazy,
People say we're crap,
That's why I want to tell you,
'Bout the teenage rap.

When I'm chilling down the park,
I won't abuse your kids,
Or beat them up,
Or sell them for the highest bids.

I've got a little sister,
She's only just two,
I take care of children,
I think they're kind of cute!

People say we're lazy,
People say we're crap,
That's why I want to tell you,
'Bout the teenage rap.

And then it comes to schoolwork,
Well yeah it's not that fun,
But I'm more likely to work,
Than be partying till one.

And sure we like a boogie,
From a phone or iPod,
But if I'm singing with my buds,
Don't glare at me like I'm odd.

People say we're lazy,
People say we're crap,
That's why I want to tell you,
'Bout the teenage rap.

I guess the fact of the matter,
Is that everyone's unique,
Thanks for this opportunity,
To let teenagers speak!

Rosie Bergonzi (14)

Silent Voice

What is the silent voice?

A conscience telling you what is right or wrong?
A voice that can never be heard outside but only within?
A whisper persuading you to listen to it?

A cry for help, but you can only hear it in your mind,
Some people choose to not listen to what it is saying,
But it will never fade away, it is always with you,
It is an inner call or a cry, the voice cannot disappear.

There are three kinds of voices, one is the angel,
Guiding you along to the right path,
It can also be a saviour or messenger from God.

The other is the Devil telling you to commit bad deeds,
It can disturb you in your dreams giving you trouble,
Haunting you with murdering screams.

The last is your own, it channels your inner thoughts,
And speaks out your mind,
But which voice should you listen to?

What is the silent voice?

Neelam Shah (15)

Love Poem

Love is a connection between two people,
Love is a key to happiness,
Love is something you cannot control,
Love is a feeling in the air,
Love is a big step in your life,
Love is a great emotion.

Love is not all what it seems,
Love is not a one person effort,
Love is not something you rescue,
Love is not always great,
Love is not what you ignore.

Love happens when you meet your lover,
Love happens when you like someone the same as they like you,
Love happens when you cannot stop thinking of someone,
Love happens when the two of you have trust for each other,
Love happens when you have a lot in common with someone,
Love happens all the time.

Love causes you to be happy,
Love causes break ups,
Love causes changes to your future,
Love causes sadness to some,
Love causes a lot.

Love is many things,
Love is not simple,
Love happens to many,
Love can cause anything,
Love is great,
Love is everything.

Danny Morris (13)
Archbishop Lanfranc School, Croydon

Love

It comes from your heart,
It grows and grows and fills your heart,
It shines and gets brighter when it is shared,
It is something that shines inside you,
It's like a bright light that shines upon a loved one.

It makes the world a better place,
It belongs to the world,
It is a wonderful moment in life,
It is shared with someone special,
It is something that is special to everyone.

It shows when you give a beautiful smile,
It is given to you when you give it back,
It is when a knot is tied,
It is about enjoyment and having great days together,
It is something that your parents give you when you're born.

It goes with you everywhere,
It never leaves you,
It is part of you,
It is something that can never be broken,
It is given to everyone.

It is a word that can never be forgotten,
It is a word that is remembered by everyone,
It is something that makes you happy when it is said to you,
It is something that costs nothing,
Love.

Tanith MacDuff-Watts (13)
Archbishop Lanfranc School, Croydon

You Still Don't Know What You Done

This pain . . .
Do you see what you've done?
You've broken something . . .
That never again will be one.

You took it,
You shattered it,
You tore it apart,
But you still don't realise . . .
That you've broken my heart.

I cry every night now,
I cry for you,
This dark cloud around me,
It's blocking me from seeing through.

My feelings are pushed aside,
My faith in you, gone,
I never realised it would come to this,
I'm sorry . . . but I'm done.

I see through these stupid lies,
I realised now what a fool I've been,
To put my heart in your hands . . .
I feel like I committed a sin.

You still don't realise . . .
How much you hurt me . . .
How much I still care . . .
You still don't realise . . .
After all you've done . . .
That love for you in my heart is still there.

I'm broken inside,
I'm fading away,
I will never again fall for . . .
That smile on your face.

What makes me even worse . . .
Is that you still don't know . . .
I'm so hurt inside,
I know that compassion is one thing . . .
You never show.

Why did you do this?
That is my last question . . .
As I'm lying here,
It's the question . . .
Whose answer I'm dying to hear.

Please . . . tell me . . .
Why did you hurt me?
Why did you break my heart?
Please . . . answer me . . .
I know it's not hard.

Yet . . . I wish I could see you . . .
Just one last time,
I wish I could be with you,
Holding your hand in mine.

Sruthi Vaman (13)
Archbishop Lanfranc School, Croydon

My Poem

We walk out,
You try to touch me,
I shrug you off,
I want to scream but my rage stops me.

She comes out,
She tries to run away,
You stop her,
I look at you with disgust.

You both cross the road,
I walk on the other side,
Both of you laugh,
A piece of me dies.

I go home,
It's lonely now,
The thought of you *two*,
Makes me want to die.

Moeez Khan (13)
Archbishop Lanfranc School, Croydon

Love Is Like . . .

Love is like a writer's pen hitting paper,
Love is like the North and South Pole attracting,
Love is like the sun shining on a summer's day,
Love is like . . .
Love is like a chocolate bar,
Hard on the outside but soft on the inside,
Love is like a pencil, it can snap at any time,
Love is like a cushion comforting you to sleep,
Love is like . . .
Love is like a band playing music,
If one person messes up, they all mess up,
Love is like . . .

Tyrrell O'Dame (13)
Archbishop Lanfranc School, Croydon

Choices

I am at the crossroads in my life,
Should I study or pick up a knife?
I don't know what to do,
Should I join a book club or join a crew?
What's at the end of the road I'll take?
Is it worth putting my life at stake?
My mind is confused, I'm twisted inside,
I feel battered and bruised,
It doesn't make sense,
I can't loosen up,
I'm always tense.

Reece Muir (14)
Archbishop Lanfranc School, Croydon

Love

Love is four letters of dedication,
Love begins a journey of life,
Love is a fan club for two members only,
Love is when you find your soulmate,
Love is a romantic bond between two people,
Love resembles trust and friendship,
Love is something you can't help,
Love is the key to happiness,
Love has a meaning so never forget it,
Love is something not to hide away,
Love is a journey we all must take,
Love is a word with no age restriction,
Love appears when you least expect it,
Love can make and break you,
Love is a power, good and bad,
Love is something no one else can choose,
Love is the feeling no one can predict,
Love is a power beyond control,
Love is a word that comes from the heart,
Love is a heart full of sad and happy times ahead,
Love is a ride with lots of ups and downs,
Love will take anyone without an invitation,
Love happens at first sight,
Love is a hand that grips the heart,
Love is a light that overpowers the dark,
Love will bring you out of the dark,
And into the light . . .

James Lundy (13)
Archbishop Lanfranc School, Croydon

Love Poem

Boy's point of view
If only I had showed you some love and affection,
If only I had spoken to you in the morning,
If only I was on time to pick up the phone to have a romantic talk,
If only I was there at the Nativity of your child,
If only I was there to show you the passion on our anniversary,
If only I could just pick up the phone and express the way
                                                    I feel for you,
If only you and I could go out and have a one to one.

Girl's point of view
Why couldn't you just be there for me when I needed someone
                                            the most?
Why couldn't you just make an effort to show me a bit
                                of love and affection?
Why couldn't you just love me when we were talking to each other?
Why couldn't you just talk to me when we came
                    transversely towards each other?
Why couldn't you just pick up the phone and just talk
                        to me like normal couples.

Brandon Fabian Baynes (13)
Archbishop Lanfranc School, Croydon

My Life

Every day I have a pain in my ears and eyes,
'Do this!' 'Do that!' my life is controlled in many ways,
My mum, my family, even my mates,
What is the point of life, when you get bossed around?
I might as well die, jump off a building or jump in front of a car,
I might as well die!

Chanel Micallef (11)
Archbishop Lanfranc School, Croydon

The Market Thief

Bizarre, laree, the smell leering through,
Objects of gold, silver and the odd thing new,
You go to observe, to deter a mind's dawdle,
Fake watches, matches, such unending hue.

The advertisers call, the cheap-cooked food,
Spices galore,
Devices a-shored,
Prices for sure,
This suffices.

Slithering through the heat lies the market thief,
His air of authority over every stall,
No one dare accuse,
For he alone knows how to use.

Every market rule in the book,
Enjoy your gold and silver,
But watch your pockets,
He loves all those valuable lockets.

Does he live in you?

Antony Mears (16)
Bexhill High School, Bexhill-on-Sea

Betrayal

The desolate landscape scarred by war lay dormant . . .

Two ditches carved into the barren countryside,
Razor like wire sat majestically in-between the two trenches,
The decayed remains of noble men hung off it in strips,
Brown soil painted a dark scarlet,
And green, green grass speckled with spots of ruby,
Puddles of stagnant water and gold lay on the field,
A man laid, defeated by agony, with gold oozing from him,
His jewels were failing as his eyes turned to ice,
A metallic rattle sounded,
The highly explosive pellets aimed at advancing ranks,
The thud of pellets against flesh and bone,
Spots, drops and puddles of gold were flying in all directions,
Silver and platinum pools were forming around the mass of corpses,
One fatality lay with half of his thinkin' cap hanging out,
Its silver surface gleaming,
He was not the only one,
Death would not mar the charge for victory.

5 years later.

A ruthless murderer stood facing his office window,
The pale lime walls stained yellow by the smoky haze,
His broad frame wore an expensive suit,
A sack of money sat on his mahogany desk,
Victory in the First World War had led to a bonus,
As he greedily shook open the bag a pool of dark red
Liquor emerged on his desk . . .

Ben Elphick (16)
Bexhill High School, Bexhill-on-Sea

This Place

Mud, blood and decay battered their senses,
Death's barbed claws tore at them,
Poison's icy tentacles smothered them,
The night stole their hope,
The dark stole all mercy,
Men turned into boys and boys turned into ghosts,
Bombs exploded,
Humans shouted,
Bodies mangled,
Souls destroyed,
And all the while they crouched,
They crouched and shivered and waited,
They waited in the dark,
In the dark and damp and ice,
For the shells they waited, whistling and whining,
For the guns they waited, booming and tolling,
For the poison they waited, smoking and silent,
For the friends they waited, vanished and gone,
For the death they waited,
In this place,
This deadly, forsaken place,
This no hope land,
This no joy land,
This no-man's-land.

Anandi Simpkins (15)
Bexhill High School, Bexhill-on-Sea

Our Common Identity

I am who I am and what I need to be,
But you'll never lose your common identity,
We'll laugh with each other until the end of days,
But you'll go home and rot in so many different ways,
And plunder the new sensations for what you think is
Everyone's common needs,
You'll hide the fact that everyone bleeds,
Cover it up with contemporary and modern greeds,
Fuel the desire that feeds,
On these macho and slick controversies,
For you are you and what you need to be,
And I'll never forget your common identity,
Whilst you poison and recreate,
Smash down all futile debates,
Multiply that picture's perfect face,
A thousand of you for every race,
Metal constructs and plasma screens your base,
Fancy words, new hair and old ideas you'll face,
Any sense of hierarchy's grace,
As you guard your walls with lawyer's haste,
Burn, your humanity and sanity, offer up the sanctions,
Of common identity,
This modern so-called democracy,
A rapist's discovery,
A pauper's catastrophe,
A priest's blasphemy,
Burn our common identity,
For we're different in every way,
And when powers run and colour fades to grey,
You'll bow to God and He'll say,
'I wish I hadn't created you in that sinful way.'

Charlie Firman (16)
Bexhill High School, Bexhill-on-Sea

At Night I Dream

At night I dream of a happy place,
Where nobody ever is two-faced,
A place where we all get along,
Somewhere that you can do no wrong,
Where poverty and money is not an issue,
No sad eyes or crying into a tissue.

At night I dream of unique girls and guys,
There are no secrets, there are no lies,
People are around whom I know I can trust in,
Where your face doesn't matter it's what's from within,
Where people are inspiration their personalities are strong,
A place where all is right and never wrong.

At night I dream of a world in unity,
At night I dream of all races in a community,
At night I dream of a world without war,
With inspiration and the world in awe,
At night I dream of a happy place,
Where character matters and not your race,
At night I dream that your orientation doesn't care,
Where nothing matters how you dress or what you wear.

At night I dream that stereotypes are gone,
At night I dream that hatred was never here all along,
At night I dream that racism is wrong,
At night I dream we can all get along.

At night I have many dreams,
So many that most are so unseen,
Dreams don't lie and so I'll tell you,
My biggest dream is that all my dreams come true.

Clare Holman-Hobbs (16)
Bexhill High School, Bexhill-on-Sea

Blissful Ignorance . . .

Blissful ignorance tearing at my seams,
I swarm from the jungle of childish dreams,
Through the corridors littered with pleasure,
Till I greet the face stating 'It's merely begun'.

We wade across the hype of the playground,
Inane and naïve as words can't be found,
Struck by the news delivered with pity,
Oblivious, for years, I chose t'remain.

Watching the replays, over and over,
Counting the seconds till each one collapsed,
I can remember flicking the channels,
Eager to escape, I yearned to relax.

These twin beams of light, suddenly scattered,
That and my world each falling down,
Those two neighbours I once loved so dearly,
Feuding with fury, in anger they'll drown.

The taste of these days too bitter t'savour,
The chaos it caused I'll never forgive,
This burden, heavy, upon my shoulders,
Now it's subsiding, perhaps I can live.

Mary Haymaker (15)
Bexhill High School, Bexhill-on-Sea

Mr Businessman

Well hello there Mr Businessman,
How did you get up there?
With your designer leather briefcase,
And side-parting in your hair.

But may I ask you Sir,
How many people did you use?
Stabbing them in the back,
And fearing what you'd lose.

Are you pleased Mr Businessman,
Sat in your classy chair,
Do you regret what you've done Sir,
Because you don't seem to care?

Was it really worth it Sir?
After all your workers slaved,
Buy some starving people food,
Maybe their lives will be saved.

I chew now on my piece of bread,
And see you with your three course meal,
Are you grateful for what you've achieved,
Because I don't think it's a fair deal.

Emma Meakin (15)
Bexhill High School, Bexhill-on-Sea

Untitled Love

Just hearing your voice,
I can do nothing but rejoice.

But not to have your touch,
To make my heart beat so much,

Then the day would be here,
And I cannot wait to hold you near.

But then we must depart,
To turn again to a broken heart.

Leaving your hand behind me,
Not sure of when the next time will be.

Back to simply your exquisite voice,
And once again we have but no choice.

Emily Robinson (15)
Bexhill High School, Bexhill-on-Sea

Night Butterflies

Dark is the night,
As I lay on the sodden ground,
Cold . . . cold, it was ever so slightly,
Warm, your finger drawing pictures on my bare arm,
Artistic? Like the picture that could be painted of us here,
'Your eyes sparkle like the stars in the sky,'
A cliché to some extent,
But I don't notice,
Mesmerised in the sky, the black sheet that covers us,
With the occasional speck of light, here and there,
I smile,
A chill shivers slowly up my spine,
Our eyes meet,
And like a warm blanket,
Your arms cover me,
I think I have butterflies.

Amy Deeprose (16)
Bexhill High School, Bexhill-on-Sea

Brother

I remember the first time I saw you brother,
You were so tiny, you were so perfect,
I used to see you every week,
But now, it's been six months without even a glance,
And I'm scared, scared that in ten years or so,
You won't even know who I am,
I'll lose you,
Just like I lost our father,
All those years ago,
It's not your fault, *you are* only a baby,
It's him I blame,
He moved for his own selfish reason,
And like old times, it's the others that are left to suffer.

Alice Hampson (15)
Bexhill High School, Bexhill-on-Sea

Rhyming Poem

R hyming poems are my favourite, and better than the rest,
H aving all the fun writing them, I think they are the best,
Y apping people talking about poems,
M issing out the rhyming poem,
I love to rhyme a lot and never get tired of it,
N ever ever quit at it,
G reat fun rhyming is,

P lenty of poems with rhyming in,
O h I think that rhyming will always win,
E xtraordinary how the words rhyme,
M uch better than watching TV in my time,
S o now you have heard how great rhyming is.

Patrick Sheehy (11)
Blenheim High School, Epsom

People Poem

George has a bogey under his bed,
Abby has bubblegum on her head,
Ollie has earwax on his shoe,
Charlotte dyed her hair bright blue.

Blaine keeps a dinosaur in her shed,
Amber has a crocodile under her bed,
Luke has a caterpillar in his pocket,
Amy sent a spider up in a rocket.

William somersaults across the floor,
Miss Ford says, 'Please no more'.
As for me, I breed bats,
But I don't like to dwell on that.

Scott Finch (11)
Blenheim High School, Epsom

Bubblegum

There's a piece of bubblegum stuck behind my ear,
I haven't really chewed on it so have I made that clear,
It may sound quite disgusting,
Please do not be mean,
It used to be bright purple but now it's gone all green!
I haven't ever spoke of it,
I am scared of people telling,
That my piece of bubblegum,
Behind my ear is dwelling.

Abigail Goodwin-Smith (11)
Blenheim High School, Epsom

Winter

Christmas is like a ray of decorations,
The snow is a sheet over the land,
Presents at Christmas under the tree,
The tree is like a stairway to Heaven.

Nice warm fires, like your house is on fire,
Candles are alight in a room,
Snowmen are like new life in the world,
Santa is a big bundle of joy.

Christmas pudding for everyone to enjoy,
Holly as prickly as a hedgehog,
Cold weather like you are in a freezer,
Presents are like a new beginning to this world.

All these things happen in winter.

Keren Bignall (11)
Blenheim High School, Epsom

School At The Beach

You may have noticed, teachers,
I am not in school today,
But the tape deck on my desk,
Will record each word you say,
Switch on my laptop's webcam,
When you have something to show,
And if you pass out homework,
Find my fax number below,
I've a pager and cellphone,
So I don't need to be in class,
I won't be hard to reach,
I'll do all the work at the beach.

Millie Fox (12)
Blenheim High School, Epsom

Winter!

The snow is cotton wool,
The cold is like snow all around us,
Christmas is your birthday for everyone,
Snowmen are people made out of snow,
Santa is like a big bundle of love,
Holly is a prickly hedgehog,
Snowballs as round as a football,
Presents wrapped are like us wrapped up for the cold,
Gloves when it's cold are like oven gloves when cooking,
The Christmas tree is like a green shooting star,
Christmas cake is cake with juicy fruit.

Emma Corrie (11)
Blenheim High School, Epsom

My Monster

It has . . .
A head like a fat football,
A body like the Empire State Building,
Ears like boats,
A mouth like a rotten old tree,
Teeth like bloody daggers,
Eyes like stingy bees,
Arms like trains out of control,
Legs like broomsticks,
Feet like rollerblades,
Hands like lightsabers cutting at buildings,
A rose like a witch's head,
Its breath smells like a pigsty,
It moves like a drunken old man,
It falls over every little step,
It has big red cuts all over.

Benjamin Wilman (11)
Blenheim High School, Epsom

My Old Bogey

My old bogey,
Sitting under my bed,
I know you won't believe me,
But it's the size of the shed.

I know you won't believe this,
I promise I've never lied,
I showed my sister my horrid green bogey,
And she really almost died.

If my bogey's growing,
I wonder every day,
I think about it every night,
While in bed I lay.

I love my bogey very much,
I hug it every day,
That as my homework art project,
I'll make it out of clay.

Yesterday the Royal Duke,
Came to stay for tea,
I showed him my old green bogey,
And it really made him puke.

Later that evening,
Mum broke my heart,
She popped my green bogey by chucking a dart,
My bogey shrunk and shrivelled up, I thought Mum wouldn't dare,
So, I got a piece of bubblegum,
And stuck that under there.

George Hemmings (11)
Blenheim High School, Epsom

The World

If I ruled the world,
I would turn the sky into a pink pool,
Where I can swim forever on and on.

If I ruled the world,
I would climb the highest mountain,
Until I've reached the stars so high.

If I ruled the world,
I would collect all the food in the world,
And help the famished people who need food.

If I ruled the world,
I would fly over the seas,
And say 'Hello' to the flying birds.

If I ruled the world,
I would turn the sun purple,
And the moon would be blue.

If I ruled the world,
I would own all the clothes in the world,
Including my favourite shoes.

If I ruled the world,
I would make sure there was no homework,
And I'd get rid of the subjects I hate.

If I ruled the world,
I would help my friends in need,
And stay with the people I love.

Katherine Holloway (11)
Blenheim High School, Epsom

A Bolt Of Lightning

A loud sudden noise that draws your attention,
A bright spark just like a camera flashing,
Like a two battled war between two armies,
But still the thunder is pondering and wandering.

Faye Hardy (11)
Blenheim High School, Epsom

My Marvellous Monster

A head as big as a football pitch,
A body as round as a plate,
Ears as long as a trumpet,
Eyes the colour of slate.

A nose as red as a cherry,
Teeth as yellow as chips,
Hair as green as spinach,
Arms as wide as great ships.

Claws as sharp as a needle,
Legs as brown as mud,
A tail as thick as a piece of rope,
Fingers as red as blood.

My monster's more spotty than leopards,
He smells like a row of old bins,
He's as batty as a nutty professor,
On a Sunday he wears his shark fins.

If you see my old monster near Blenheim,
Keep him clear of the caretaker's shed,
Send him straight back to my granny's,
Where he lives underneath her old bed.

Eleanor Friston (11)
Blenheim High School, Epsom

Winter

Christmas is like a shiny star,
Winter is like an icy storm,
Winter is like a snowy day,
Santa is like a jolly bunny,
Presents are like a crystal light of happiness,
Gloves are like a snug fire,
A snowman is like a still statue,
Holly is like prickly teeth.

Josiah Odimah-Manson (11)
Blenheim High School, Epsom

I'm A Peace Dove

As I'm high up in the cloudy sky,
The wind ruffling my cover,
Staring down at the tiny specs of colour beneath me.

I see the tall shadow of the figure as I'm looking down,
And look up again to see the wide feature ahead,
Slowly I flap and flip, then land gracefully as possible.

As I perch upon my chosen brown metre,
I bound as I thoughtfully think,
About the peace I'm about to grant.

As my snow body takes flight,
I land again on a feature that is taller than the tree,
And slide slowly down.

I'm on a grey surface now,
And see the tiny specs of colour grow bigger and bigger,
I try to hop and jump as one comes towards me,
But my wings let me down.

A strange barred box falls over me,
And a black shadow looms,
There is nothing to hear but an eerie silence and the box lifts off.

I feel freedom and fly high,
At last, once again,
The breeze let's me flop and float.

Ilar Bristo (11)
Blenheim High School, Epsom

If I Was The Queen . . .

If I were the queen, I would make boys disappear,
If I were the queen, I would tell all teachers not to give out homework,
If I were the queen, I would turn everything into chocolate,
And I would eat it whenever I wanted,
If I were the queen, I would wish and wish till I got all these things,
If I were the queen, I would have my sister as a slave,
Oh, I wish I were the queen.

Sammy Neal
Blenheim High School, Epsom

A Poem About My Cat Sherbert

M y cat Sherbert is two days younger than me,
Y ummy she thinks when I give her some food.

C uddles I give her when I come home,
A round the garden she chases the leaves,
T hrough the window she keeps a lookout.

S herbert is playful while I try to work,
H appy to sleep while I am at school,
E very morning she wakes me up which helps,
R unning wild when fireworks are banging,
B ut she is calm when I give her some milk,
E ven when it's pouring, she wants to go outside,
R eally, really black all over with one white spot,
T errific and purrrrfect, my cat Sherbert.

Scott Dance (11)
Blenheim High School, Epsom

Jungle Poem

Treacherous tigers catching their prey,
Lazy lions sleeping all day,
Excitable monkeys swinging through trees,
And baby baboons doing just as they please.

Bouncy tree frogs croaking and hopping,
Marvellous macaws fly without stopping,
Huge hefty hippos thumping along,
The Sangha Forest robin singing his song.

The jungle I think is the best place to be,
With so much to do and so much to see,
Wonderful animals all sizes and shapes,
What's sad is mankind will decide on its fate.

Charlotte Ayley-Poulter (11)
Blenheim High School, Epsom

Monster In My Room

Does your bedroom have monsters,
That come out late at night?
And does your wallpaper have faces,
Which appear when your mum turns out the light?
And from your wardrobe can you hear whispers,
A strange silent kind of noise?
But the scariest of all,
Are the faces on your toys,
But when you put the light on,
Do the monsters go away?
Is the wallpaper just wallpaper,
And do the noises have no more to say?
The reason things are different,
I am sure that you will find,
Is when you realise they were never there,
They were always just in your mind.

George Ackerman (12)
Blenheim High School, Epsom

My Monster Poem

It has:
A body like a frying pan,
A head like a cactus,
Ears like two pencils that are blunt,
A mouth like a pretty blue flower,
Teeth like two red tomatoes,
Eyes like two ticking clocks,
Legs and arms like bright yellow bananas,
Claws like round tennis balls,
And a tail like a winding skipping rope.

Amy Cotton (11)
Blenheim High School, Epsom

The School

School is a dragon, large and scary,
Windows are clear glass bottles,
Doors are redwood trees,
This school is as big as a city.

I want to be a lion, brave and strong,
As I walk through the doors but inside I feel like a wobbly jelly,
One deep breath, head held high,
I take the plunge as I dive through the doors,
Every minute is a decade long,
School's a life sentence, will I survive?

What a fuss, so much worry!
All the rain clouds have gone,
Sun shines in my mind,
Friends are flowers growing around me,
Teachers are a box of tools with instructions there to help me,
The day is done,
The dragon's dead,
I am a bird flying home to my nest.

Charlotte White (12)
Blenheim High School, Epsom

Autumn

The leaves are multicoloured snowflakes falling to the ground,
The fireworks are like red jets flying through the sky,
The mornings are a blackness that never turns light,
People are in their costumes like they are shedding their skin,
Showing their true form,
The fire is a raging bull of red keeping us warm,
The pumpkin is a circular monster waiting to kill,
All these things happen in autumn.

Luke Adam Charlton (11)
Blenheim High School, Epsom

Smiles

A smile is like . . .
A rainbow during a shower of rain,
A sunset full of vibrant colour,
The smell of rain after a summer monsoon,
Silky sand running through your fingers.

A parent's embrace,
A bird flying over a sunset sky,
Hearing your favourite CD,
A finished work of art,
A mug of indulgent cocoa after a walk on a clear autumn evening,
A piece of triple berry pie,
Receiving an A on a test,
Your best friend giving you a much needed hug,
A glistening spiderweb caught on a dewy morning,
Snuggled under the duvet with your favourite book,
Finding the last piece of a puzzle,
The phone call you've been waiting for,
A clean white sheet of paper waiting to be written on,
Sleeping in on a weekend morning,
That's what makes me smile.

Emily Hughes (11)
Blenheim High School, Epsom

A World Of The Future

The future is a mile away,
It takes about a year and a day,
You think about what will happen to you,
And about who will marry you!

Will the future be bad?
Will the future be good?

I wonder what the future holds,
Dreaming of what will happen to me and you!

Laura Evans (11)
Blenheim High School, Epsom

Computers, Computers

Computers, computers, boy aren't they fun,
I like the games when you're on the run with a gun,
It's clever but it's also dumb,
Sometimes I hurt my thumb.

Computers, computers, boy aren't they cool,
There are even computers at school,
You get to surf the Net,
And get a virtual pet.

Computers, computers, boy aren't they quick,
I spend all day going *click, click, click,*
The only bit I don't like is the homework,
Whoever invented it is a definite jerk!

Bradley Smith (11)
Blenheim High School, Epsom

My Naughty Cat

Meet my cat Barney,
He is very quiet even though he will make a riot,
He will scream if we go to the vets in Cheam,
When my cat goes on my bed,
My dad gets very red,
He thinks he is cattle or a baby with a rattle,
If there isn't a speck of food,
You don't want to see him in his *hungry* mood,
Meet my cat Barney, as he is sleeping on my lap calmly.

Brooke Doughorty (11)
Blenheim High School, Epsom

Teenagers

T eenagers hang around after school,
E nough of them around,
E njoying all the different privileges,
N oise as they talk and laugh together,
A ttitudes that parents hate,
G oing to libraries to study for their A Levels,
E xciting and new experiences they will have,
R ushing to get out of school and move on,
S o enjoy it while it lasts.

Samuel Cates (11)
Blenheim High School, Epsom

Chelsea!

My favourite team is Chelsea,
Stamford Bridge is where they play,
The home strip is blue
And yellow when away.

John Terry is the captain,
The best player of them all,
He plays at centre back,
And always wins the ball.

We have lots of money,
And always buy the best,
This season will be hard,
But we will pass the test.

Champions Lgeague winners,
That would be a dream,
I am sure Chelsea can do it,
My favourite football team.

Charlie Lyon (11)
Blenheim High School, Epsom

Winter

Winter is as cold as a freezer and fridge put together,
Gloves to keep you warm,
Christmas pudding as hot as a blowtorch,
Snow looks like ice cream,
Hat to keep your head warm,
Christmas Day comes, getting lots of presents,
Snow as white as a swan,
Play snowball fights all day long,
I feel sad when it is all gone.

Aaron Riches (12)
Blenheim High School, Epsom

My Generation

Bang, bang, you're dead,
I wonder if the reliable NHS will have a bed?
Playing with his friends,
As the bullet bounced off a Mercedes Benz.

The wheels on the bike go round and round,
Will the gunman ever be found?
As this poor little boy lay dead on the ground.

Only 11, and killed by an AK47,
I wonder if he will go to Heaven,
Is this gunman in a gang?
What normal person would do this to
An 11-year-old boy?

Bang, bang.

Denver Miller (13)
Glyn Technology School, Epsom

The Environment

The more you drive,
The less you stay alive,
Global warming is a curse,
It is still getting worse.

We need to recycle,
So use a bicycle,
Recycle those plastic and metal cans,
So we can make new pots and pans,
Glass jars, plastic bottles, anything goes,
So that we can make a new hose.

We're cutting down the trees,
It's affecting the birds and bees,
Lots of animals are losing their homes,
They're being left to die alone,
So for every tree that gets cut
Another should be put up.

Let's go inside our homes,
Lots of things we need to change,
We must try to rearrange.

Do not turn the switches on again and again,
Otherwise when you see the bill you will be in pain,
When you wash your clothes,
Bring down the temperature to 30 degrees,
Come on let's save the world, please!

Ata Chaudhry (11)
Glyn Technology School, Epsom

The Environment

If we don't do something,
Our lives could end,
To stop this fate,
Our ways we must end.

If there's litter on the floor,
Then put it in the bin,
And you could find,
It turns into a tin.

The ice caps are melting,
Because of pollution,
To stop this, we should
Do things by hand,
Cycle to work.

Every corner you turn,
There's graffiti on the wall,
Because of the hoodies,
They haven't got anything else to do.

What would we do
To save our planet?
Stop and think
Before it shrinks.

James Stone (11)
Glyn Technology School, Epsom

The Future

It's great being a child at this time,
But that's the present, what about the future?
Global warming is causing problems,
In less than twenty years countries will sink,
What if I can't live in the future?
What if I go down with the countries?
Down with my homeland?
It saddens me thinking about it,
But I just can't stop,
Many things might happen in the future,
World War III, floods,
But what if there's a cure?
What if America and Iraq get along?
What if we stop polluting the air?
Why don't people understand?
Why do they laugh when I talk about the future?
At night I can't sleep,
Thinking about the future and present,
Why is the world like this?
Why did we start these things?
Why couldn't we make a better future?
But can I only think in the present?
I can't change the future.

Ekrem Yuksel Demeni (11)
Glyn Technology School, Epsom

My Generation

My friends and family are important to me,
They are there to help me when I need help,
I am there for them when they need help,
I love my friends and family all so much.

Sports are also very important to me,
Like football, cricket and rugby,
The way the injuries happen,
The way the sweat drips,
The way the tackles happen.

The television is very important to me,
How often I watch it, how often I enjoy it,
All of the television shows,
How I relax on the sofa and enjoy.

The polluted world is another thing,
The way we should look after our world,
Get public transport instead of cars,
Do not smoke in public places.

My things that I own are also very special to me,
I make sure that I look after my personal things,
So I do not lose them, I love most things I have,
But mostly God gave me a life and I am very grateful.

Alex Malyon (11)
Glyn Technology School, Epsom

30 Seconds

Children playing, swinging and running,
Parents talking on the benches of the park, laughing away,
People working, enjoying their lives,
30 seconds left,
Couples sitting and having a romantic dinner, not knowing,
Teachers teaching misbehaving children,
Children messing about, having fun, not knowing . . .
20 seconds left,
Families having picnics,
People swimming with their friends,
People eating while others starve,
Families uniting,
10 seconds left,
Babies being born, the miracle of life,
9 seconds left,
Old, worn-out people fading away,
8 seconds left,
People sleeping peacefully,
7 seconds left,
The patient lying in her hospital bed while the
Cancer is eating her away,
6 seconds left,
Animals fleeing for their lives,
5 seconds,
Babies crying knowing what's going to happen,
4 seconds left,
People living peacefully,
3 seconds left,
Children making friends,
2 seconds,
Angels watching over us,
1 second left,
Out of time, dead.

Cayden Nel (13)
Glyn Technology School, Epsom

School Poem

As I walk through the rusty black gates
That suck me into a different world,
I can see through the black gates,
Fun, but where I am?
I see boredom and a world of learning,
A world I don't want to be in.

While in science, I'm not thinking chemistry,
Instead I'm thinking of football and I pour in different
Chemicals into a beaker,
I think of myself scoring the winning goal
And as the bell rings,
I am thinking of the final whistle blowing
And my dad clapping us all off the pitch.

While in maths, I'm not thinking of addition,
I think of the scoreboard changing from three-nil to four,
And when I get a high maths result,
I think of our team captain lifting up the league cup,
When instead I'm only in maths.

When I'm in geography I'm not thinking of the longest river,
Instead I'm thinking of all the different football teams of the world,
Or when we're looking at landmarks,
I'm thinking of all the stadiums,
Wishing one day I could be there and be as
Famous as David Beckham.

When I'm in history, I'm supposed to be thinking
Of the Roman Empire,
And about the war between the Celts,
When in fact, I'm thinking of the tragic accident
Of Man Utd in Munich.

There's only one problem,
When I'm thinking of football,
My mind is in a different place,
It's in the world of fun when I'm actually in the world of learning,
And as soon as the bell rings, well,
That's when the real fun begins.

Dimitri Constantinou (12)
Glyn Technology School, Epsom

Now!

Too much TV makes my mind feel hollow,
Too many computers make me weep with sorrow,
Too many parties make my head bang like a drum,
Too many deaths take away all my fun,
All of the motorists give me a fright,
And my noisy neighbours keep me up all night,
So much chewing gum litters my street,
And no one walks or uses their feet,
The climate is changing and so are the youths,
Please keep them away from the cash booths!
(Mavis, 81)

Music is my lifeline, it keeps me going strong,
Gossip is my saviour, it makes my mind last long,
Make-up is my happiness, it hides all the bad,
And sweets will make me hyper, then I will feel sad,
Going to parties means I never sleep,
But I don't mind because of the friends that I keep,
Going to the gym keeps me fit,
I like to keep active and won't learn to knit,
Breaking the rules is my aim in life,
But I'm not so stupid that I would use a knife!
(Zoe, 15)

I watch the race cars whizzing by,
And in a plane, I can fly so high,
I've always wanted to own a boat,
So in the sea we can race and float,
I love my dog, his name is Jasper,
And I thank my school called St Casper's,
I've been to Uni. and I've got a job,
And I have a flatmate whose name is Bob,
I look to the future and hope to have a wife,
But I will always look to my mother for advice!
(Tony, 23)

Nicky Britton-Williams (13)
Gordon's School, Woking

What I Love Best

I love to laugh, to giggle out loud,
My days of sorrow are over, I've vowed,
Goodbye grief, morning, sadness and distress,
Enjoying this new feeling I've come to possess!

Bright, sunny days in the glorious spring,
It's amazing how much joy small things can bring,
The trickle of water, the sweep of the breeze,
And of course all the flowers, making me sneeze!

Reading in a deckchair, relaxed in the shade,
In the centre of a meadow, in a peaceful glade,
With the sun shining on me, I'm warm as can be,
To stay here forever is my one and only plea.

In a blissful park, calmly eating a cake,
Whilst feeding some bread to the ducks in the lake,
The ripeness of jam and the creaminess of butter,
And the many birds flying the skies in a flutter.

Another thing I adore is visiting the funfair,
Racing down rides, having braids in my hair,
The sense of freedom, life and thrill,
It's all so amazing and must take skill!

My home is safe; it's where I belong,
My family are there - they keep me strong,
It's warm, so cosy and the place I can find,
Filled with love, affection and smiles combined!

Amira Arasteh (13)
Gordon's School, Woking

My Generation

My generation,
Has no concentration,
Distractions here, distractions there.

Hair from spiked to long,
From black to blond.

The only grades we want to see,
It's only the Nintendo Wii.

There are so many different trends,
Drive me around the bend.

Will I stand out
Or will I raise a shout?

From chav to emo,
Shrek or Nemo,
Which one will I choose?

James Watson (11)
Hazelwick School, Crawley

My Generation

Technology is ever changing,
Excitement all around,
iPods playing downloads,
Online shopping safe and sound.

Games for PCs, PlayStations and the other lot,
Children wanting Heelys,
Parents losing the plot!

Jess Grist (11)
Hazelwick School, Crawley

My Poem

Hi my name is Jade,
I'm 11-years-old,
And I'm as good as gold.

My mum thinks I'm sweet,
And very good,
And I always try to do as I should.

I have a brother called Matt,
He is sometimes fun,
But we often fight,
Like most kids have done.

I have a hamster called Biggles,
He often gives me lots of giggles,
He is very old and won't live long,
But I will miss him lots when he is gone.

Jade Coulstock (11)
Hazelwick School, Crawley

Friendship

Friends can help when you're new,
They cheer you up when you're feeling blue,
They help when homework gets too hard,
They make you a special birthday card.

Sharing, gossip and secrets are fun,
Or just being lazy in the sun,
A friend to go shopping with you,
Then you get the deal 3 for 2.

Sophie Tubb (11)
Hazelwick School, Crawley

My Generation

My life has had many changes,
But this is the biggest one of all,
Apparently it's quite different from my mum's,
Especially from when she was small.

From the toys that she used to play with,
To the places she went as a kid,
For instance I own my own PC,
My mum used a pen with a nib!

When I need a lift to a friend's house,
Or picking up from school,
I just dial up my mum from my mobile,
But she didn't have one at all.

We both enjoy similar music,
That's one thing that has stayed the same,
We just argue over who's got the CDs,
Though Mum thinks hers were more tame!

Josh Wells (11)
Hazelwick School, Crawley

Our Environment

Our environment means everything to some people,
Anyone can change it, if they want to,
People shouldn't take it for granted,
Everyone should respect it and take care of it,
People should make it the best they can,
Everyone should recycle,
People should not pollute as much,
Everyone should not litter,
And most of all, everyone should admire our environment.

Adesh Ajmani (11)
Hazelwick School, Crawley

My First Day At School

My first day at school, I will not forget,
The entire classroom steered clear,
I had no friends, no soul, no help and no teacher!
Came close to stop what was recurred again,
Any time when someone flashed eyes on me,
They would then feel what I tried to conceal,
'Twas lunch and in the dark corner, I sole,
Mourned forcefully from pain in my stout heart,
Next, maths. The harsh dogs bark louder and then
The work becomes harder to deal with as
The harsh dogs bark even louder. Fearful.
My last lesson, seconds away from being over,
They will go to their doghouse,
I am ecstatic, sparkling, thrilled. It ended.

Viqas Hussain (15)
Hazelwick School, Crawley

Go Kids

My generation,
Boys and girls around the nation,
Some rich, some poor,
Some good, some bad,
Some happy, some sad,
Some kind of mad.

Find us at schools,
We must be fools,
We would prefer to be at the park,
When it's very, very dark.

The headmaster moans about mobile phones,
He thinks we should be recycling,
'Enjoy it while you can,' he says,
'It won't last forever.'

One day my generation will rule the world!

Nicola Stevens (11)
Hazelwick School, Crawley

Through The Eyes Of Rune

(Our rescued greyhound)

I was born as a normal greyhound,
A playful puppy that was free and could do anything,
It changed when I was chosen to race,
Everything changed, I was ignored,
And I didn't even have a proper bed to lie on at night,
I had to race: I wasn't given a choice,
I stood there behind the bars ready to race
And chase that rabbit, but I only ever won 4 times,
I practised once a day, and then I was put back in my kennel,
I only raced for a year, and then I had to retire,
I kept pulling a muscle in my leg, and lost a claw,
I got to rest and heal my leg, but I kept getting raced again,
But that day finally came, when I stopped racing
And was put in a greyhound kennel,
I stayed there, until someone wanted to re-home me,
That day finally came, when a family actually wanted me
And took me home,
I wasn't too sure at first because I didn't know what
They were going to do to me,
Even though I have been there a few weeks,
I'm still a bit nervous and don't know what the
Other dog could do to me,
But I'm glad I have a home, and a bed to sleep on,
I'm happy and they're happy so that's all that matters.

Alanna Hyatt (11)
Hazelwick School, Crawley

Celeb!

On my jet,
Heading to Hollywood,
I'm being treated like
Any star should.

Stylist's getting frantic,
Choosing my bling,
Eventually they settle,
On a *huge* diamond ring!

I check on my make-up,
And make sure I look,
Like a beautiful lady,
In a fairy tale book.

I'll practise my lines,
Then ring up my friends,
And tell them I bought,
A new Mercedes Benz!

Finally we land,
And I get out the plane,
I wave to fans,
Who are screaming my name.

I walk through the crowd,
And get in the car,
I say bye to my fans,
And drive away far.

Jessica Grinsted (11)
Hazelwick School, Crawley

School Days

We stroll around the playground,
Waiting for the bell to go,
We do our English,
Maths and science,
Hooray it's time for lunch.

Boys go and play their football,
While girls laugh and giggle,
Oh no, the bell has rung again,
It's time for French and history.

I'm tired now,
I want to go home,
The clock ticks, 3.35,
The bell rings,
Finally it's time to go,
I meet my friends,
Then we all walk home.

Avneet Chahal (11)
Hazelwick School, Crawley

Fighting In My Generation

Fighting, fighting,
What's the purpose
Of the fighting?
Life, life,
What's the purpose of life?
Fighting, fighting,
In our generation,
Life, life,
What's the purpose of life?

Kieran Howard (11)
Hazelwick School, Crawley

The F.I.E.L.D!

I'm standing here amongst the field,
Full of golden daffodils,
Children are jumping,
Clouds are pumping,
Up high in the lovely blue sky,
The sun is bright,
I'm holding a kite . . .

The lush green grass,
Is smelling so fresh,
The sun is shining,
Babies are whining.

Children are settling,
The sun has turned red,
The fun is over,
It's time for bed.

Camille Alibert (11)
Hazelwick School, Crawley

Dear Abandoner . . .

Dear Abandoner . . . how could you?
How could you? How could you?
Let its tears fall in front of your very eyes,
How could you?
How it must feel to glance at its drooping ears,
Just sitting there staring at you,
How it must feel,
How it must sound to listen to its helpless whines,
Squealing and shivering in the rain,
How it must sound,
And all you do is walk away,
How could you Abandoner?
How could you?

Molly Billyeald (11)
Hazelwick School, Crawley

Save The Polar Bears!

Polar bears are the best but very soon there'll be none left,
The world is heating up as we aren't doing enough,
The ice caps are melting and the water is arising.
The cars are driving here and there, but really no one seems to care,
Pollution is in the air, spreading everywhere,
So get right off that lousy sofa and
Keep that world going on for longer!

Abigail Crossland-Otter (11)
Hazelwick School, Crawley

My Poem

We are the next generation,
Training for our occupation,
We like to play around,
Not getting homebound.

We are the next generation,
Training for our occupation,
Going to school,
While our parents hit the pool.

We are the next generation,
Training for our occupation,
Our generation,
Is part of every nation.

We are the next generation,
Training for our occupation,
Our generation,
Has the best reputation.

We are the next generation,
Training for our occupation,
I must say goodbye,
But with a great sigh.

Daniel Gstrein (11)
Hazelwick School, Crawley

My Generation

My generation is a computer nation,
We like iPods, Wiis, PSPs and PlayStations.

My mum says you are what you eat,
I'm allowed a Double Decker but only as a treat,
I also like my Maccy D's,
But she would rather me eat more peas!

My friends and I like football and cricket,
I play midfield and when I bowl,
I try and hit the wicket.

My generation is taught to recycle,
We shouldn't drive a car but ride a bicycle.

My generation use mobiles to call and text,
The way the future's going,
Who's knows what's next?

Conor Golding (11)
Hazelwick School, Crawley

My Generation

M otions, emotions
Y ou do not know

G enerous
E nergetic
N othing we do not know
E xciting
R eality
A ll
T ime
I n
O ur
N ation.

Alexander Aherne (11)
Hazelwick School, Crawley

Long School Days

We walk around,
Laughing and giggling,
Going to school learning and working,
Girls wishing they're in control,
Boys wishing they were famous at football.

The bell goes,
We run out screaming,
Break, break,
Laughing and joking,
Boys play footie,
Girls just gossip,
Argh noo,
The bell has gone,
We have to go and do some art.

We finish school,
Hip hip hooray,
We meet our friends,
Go to the park,
Got to rush home, it's getting dark.

Paige Campbell-Farrow (11)
Hazelwick School, Crawley

The Wheelchair

Cold metal,
We are two,
People stare, glare,
'Poor soul in the chair,'
A stormy symbiosis.

A ship is sunk without its sails,
It fails,
As would a bird with torn wings,
Crash and burn, the infirmed, that's me,
Live with it.

Dawn, chair,
Dusk, bed,
We're dead.
We are separated in the warm night,
But the cold morning brings us together,
Rising sun, I loathe you.

I am tied to this mast, the sirens are calling,
I am tied to this mast, the sirens are screaming.

Timothy Child (17)
Helenswood School, St Leonards-on-Sea

The Invisible Girl

She stumbles in the hallways,
Her shoes tippy-tapping,
Nobody seems to notice her,
Especially those that are yapping;
Some stare and give her evil looks,
But she's used to it by now,
She takes the abuse and punches,
Because she doesn't like to row,
She is never noticed,
And no one knows her name,
They just make her cry a lot,
As though it is a game,
She makes sure no one sees her,
When she's afraid or when she cries,
Yet no one seems to care about,
What she hides inside.

Jasmine Thorpe (13)
Helenswood School, St Leonards-on-Sea

Mistakes

I can say sorry once,
But it won't make up for what I have done,
I can say sorry a million times,
Until out of the sky falls the sun.

I can say sorry, again and again,
But I still don't deserve to be forgiven,
I can apologise and cry,
Until it's to madness I'm driven.

I can cry a thousand tears,
But still no difference would it make,
I can cry a thousand more,
But it won't compare to your heartache.

Anastasia Matvienko (15)
Helenswood School, St Leonards-on-Sea

All There Is To See

(This poem was written in memory and honour of all the homeless children who have died of disease or starvation)

Sitting on our own,
In a dirty back street,
All there is to see,
Is our horrid blackened feet.

Our parents died of hunger,
Long, long ago,
We can't get education,
So there's not much we know.

Sitting on our own,
In a dirty back street,
All there is to see,
Is our horrid blackened feet.

We dream of warmth and shelter,
Somewhere safe to live in,
With kind and healthy family,
Where lots of love is given.

Sitting on our own,
In a dirty back street,
All there is to see,
Is our horrid blackened feet.

That is what we dream of,
Every day and night,
All we want to happen,
Is for that dream to take flight.

Isabel Miller (11)
Millais School, Horsham

In A Girl's Head

In it there is her boyfriend,
And a pair of diamond earrings,
There is a factory full of excuses,
For why she shouldn't go to school.

And there is a shopping mall,
With thousands of cute handbags.

Then there is a hamster being flushed
Down the toilet,
A whinging boy crying,
And a beach full of male celebrities.

There is a plan of all the EastEnders episodes.

There is a list of all her teachers that come from the Planet Zog.

And there are thoughts, worries of calling best friend's names.

There is a picture of her history teacher actually having a life!

A giant chocolate bar that doesn't make you fat.

I believe that a girl's head is a very strange thing,
Full of imagination and plans to ditch boyfriends.

Katie Thomson (11)
Millais School, Horsham

A Cat's Head

In it there is a fish bowl,
And a scheme,
To kill all dogs.

And there is an enormous tin
Of Whiskas cat food.

And there is
An entirely new bird,
An entirely new mouse,
An entirely new frog.

There is a heated blanket,
Made of duck feathers.

There is a head scratcher.

There is alertness.

And it just cannot be trimmed.

I believe
That only what cannot be trimmed,
Is a head.

There is much promise,
In the circumstance,
That so many cats have heads.

Caroline Hillier (11)
Millais School, Horsham

In A Dog's Head

In it there is a bone,
And a lead,
For a good long walk.

And there is a plan,
To get out of dog agility.

There is an everlasting bone.

And there is
A dog bowl,
A brush,
And some other dog to say hello to.

There is a squeaky bone,
That never stops squeaking.

And the same thoughts swim around its head.

I believe
That every dog thinks about these exact
Things every day.

These thoughts carry on every single day,
They can never be stopped,
Just like us.

Ellie Brown (11)
Millais School, Horsham

In A Cat's Head

In it are wingless birds,
And some schemes,
To get rid of those drooling dogs.

And there are thoughts of pleasure,
Of cream and milk and catnip.

And there are inventions:
A human translator,
Anti-vet sprays,
An escape pod.

There is a dish,
Of unlimited milk.

There is a soft, safe bed.

There are catchable mice.

There are plans,
To sabotage other cats.

Thoughts are wonderful things.

Nicola Miller (11)
Millais School, Horsham

A Girl's Head

In it there is a swimming pool with dolphins,
And a well-thought plan
To get Mr Right.
And there is a land,
Where maths doesn't exist.
And there are cream cake hills,
A cheese castle,
And everlasting bubblegum.
There is a multicoloured rabbit,
There is a book that never ends.
And it just can't stop growing.
I believe,
That a head never stops growing,
It may seem to stop,
But inside your imagination,
Pushes the top a little higher every day.

Stella Wright (12)
Millais School, Horsham

You Can Never Catch A Dream

Dreams are like clouds,
Forever floating in the clear blue sky,
From far away you can catch,
A glimpse of the silver lining,
As you step closer you can discover more,
But no matter how hard you try,
You can never catch a dream,

Dreams are like stars,
Twinkling at midnight,
On Earth all you can see,
Are diamonds on black velvet,
But with stars and dreams,
You never see the same thing twice.

Beth Hundleby (11)
Millais School, Horsham

A Dream

The spirit of a dream, twists itself,
Round and round my head,
It whispers across my ear,
And wanders down my bed.

That's when they meet,
He is the dream master,
Controlling dreams, happy and sad,
He stores them inside, when they're good,
And chases them away when they're bad.

Thoughts are whizzing down a lane,
So deep that I could cry,
For they are frantic, it will turn
Morning from nigh.

And then after a long time,
The morning clocks will chime.

Amy Sutlieff (11)
Millais School, Horsham

My Three Treasures In My Box Are . . .

My special cat,
Who is fluffy, cuddly and purple,
She is called Martha Harris,
Now 3 years old.

A photograph of my brother,
Edward Hartfield,
A picture in an oval frame made of plastic.

My best treasure is my lovely, cuddly, wonderful mum!

Becky Street-Hartfield (13)
Patcham House Special School, Brighton

In My Box Of 12 Years

A wonderful morning
Opening three presents before school,
A good thing for today is when I get home
And cash up on my presents,
A good this is that I will get McDonald's tonight,
An exciting thing is that my family is
Coming over to celebrate my birthday,
I will see my uncle this weekend who lives in America,
The happiness I am having today, being my special day.

Ben White (12)
Patcham House Special School, Brighton

Wasp

Buzzing round the dustbin,
Going up a tree,
With its terrible sting,
Buzzing round all it sees.

In the open window,
Makes its nest,
Crawling up my pillow,
That horrible pest.

Yellow and black,
Horrid little monster,
Buzzing in its pack.

Pointing out its stinger,
Looking like a bee,
It's going to get you,
Making people flee.

Into the living room,
Out came the newspaper,
Wasp went splat!

Charlie Warner (13)
Patcham House Special School, Brighton

The Darkness

The darkness crawls along the walls,
Leaping swiftly from wall to wall, gliding, soaring like a bird,
Perching on every tree,
Spying on its prey.

The darkness creeps,
Along my curtain,
Whispering as it goes,
Knocking on the door at night,
Spooking everyone in sight.

The darkness creeps along the corridor,
Sweeping across windows in the house,
Hiding behind the cupboard doors,
Saying boo! And you're freaked out.

Edward Street Hartfield (15)
Patcham House Special School, Brighton

My Nightmare Poem

I have a fear of spiders,
They call it arachnophobia,
I have a fear of wasps and bees,
They call it nothing,
I call it buzzophobia.

I have a fear of getting lost,
I have a fear of death,
I call it deathophobia,
I have a fear of enclosed spaces,
They call it claustrophobia,
I have a fear of seagulls.

Callum Galloway (13)
Patcham House Special School, Brighton

Retrospective Life

Alienation is one thing,
That is common in my world,
'I've given birth to a monster,' Mother says,
'She's given birth to a Munster,' I say.

I'm isolated from the others,
For my taste of 70s rock,
'He's just unique,' Mother says,
'I'm just plain weird,' I say.

I take interest in retro films,
Not like all the others,
'There's no problem with that,' Mother says,
'There's loads of problems with that,' I say.

Standing out isn't fun,
You never get on with anyone,
'Standing out is great,' Mother says,
'Standing out is terrible,' I say.

Life has been going bad now,
No one wants to talk to me,
'Things can only get better,' Mother says,
'Things can only get worse,' I say.

I'm sitting in my cosy room,
Music's playing and I'm feeling down,
'Look on the bright side,' Mother says,
'I'm looking on the dark side,' I say.

I'm chatting with my friends on Friday,
And everything's going great,
'I told you this would happen,' Mother says,
'Yeh whatever, shut up.'

Joseph Cooke (15)
Patcham House Special School, Brighton

In My Box Of 11 Years

Sadness for those times I need to remember,
Sadness for my great grandad who has died,
That time I went to Park Wood with my friend Conor,
Happiness for my cousins Lottie and Alfie
Who were born exactly five years apart.
Sadness for my dad who nearly broke his knee 8 years ago,
Joy for my nan on her 60th birthday,
Happiness for the joyous parts of my life,
The joy I am experiencing today,
All day,
Every day,
Of my life.

James Mortimore (12)
Patcham House Special School, Brighton

In My Box Of 11 Years

Sadness for when we lost our pet rabbit,
Happiness for my last World Book Day at my old school,
Niceness for my first gentle habit,
Happiness for my first invention that is really cool,
Excitement for my first roller coaster,
Happiness for my first Roald Dahl book
Amazement for our new toaster,
Fascination for interesting pictures to look at.

William Hanekom (11)
Patcham House Special School, Brighton

Football

Footballers run down the wing,
Taking on defenders is their thing,
They will take shots from really far out,
They will score without a doubt.

So many different nationalities,
Scoring goals are their specialities,
Different numbers on their shirt,
Finding the simple pass they're always alert.

There are so many legends of football,
Like George Best and Alan Ball,
They all loved the amazing game,
The glorious game of football.

James Bailey (13)
Rydon Community College, Pulborough

My Poem

My poem is about nature,
And what it means to me,
It could be about the freedom,
Of the waves upon the sea.

The sound of the wind and rain,
Falling from the sky,
Or the light and patterns,
Reflected in an eye.

It could be about animals,
Mammals, fish and birds,
But ultimately you will know,
A poem's only words.

Alex Leggett-Barrett (12)
Rydon Community College, Pulborough

Diving

I want to go diving,
In the deep Mediterranean Sea,
Smelling the salt,
Seeing the coral,
What fun that would be.

Dolphins grey and beautiful,
Ready to play,
Come and play it,
Jumping, hooray.

Seals sleek as silk,
Ready to dive,
And explore the deep blue ocean,
Catching silverfish as they thrive.

Fish all different colours,
Darting through the seaweed,
Coral fish, clownfish, colourful fish, dull fish,
How many are there? One, two, three.

Swimming with the fish,
Diving with the seals,
Playing with the dolphins,
Awesome!

Ellie Blunden (12)
Rydon Community College, Pulborough

The Dolphins

Dolphin crashing, splashing and dashing,
Sun rises as the dolphin splashes.

Dolphins splashing in the waves,
Dancing, singing, night and day,
They're smart and clean,
And shimmer and glimmer.

Nadia Aziz (12)
Rydon Community College, Pulborough

A Winner's Stroke Of Glory

'On your mark!'
I bend down and touch my curled toes,
I focus,
I feel like a ticking bomb, just waiting to explode,
I focus,
'Get set,'
Adrenaline pumps through me, like a machine gun,
A shrill whistle pierces the silence.

A waiting power from inside propels me forward,
I hang in the air for a split second,
Then I'm in a world of bubble,
I kick up and surface,
I swim,
I take three strokes, then a break,
I can see the Chinese dude falling behind,
I swim.
I feel I am being controlled,
I don't think about anything, it's instinct,
I'm coming to the 50m mark,
I swim.
Next, I plunge headfirst into a tumble turn,
My legs recoil and then thrust through the water,
I swim.
On a breath to the left I see the Chinese gaining,
I swim, I swim harder, it's going to be close . . .
One last stroke . . .
I touch the edge . . .
I've won.

George Bounds (12)
Rydon Community College, Pulborough

England Versus Canada

England versus Canada,
We will win without a doubt,
The crowd start cheering,
As the players come out.

They sing the national anthem,
The crowd have all gone quiet,
At the end of the match,
I hope there's not a riot.

Wilkinson gets speared,
But the ref did not see,
England are winning,
5-23.

The atmosphere's amazing,
Lewsey gets the ball,
He runs into a Canadian,
And sets up a mall.

A Mexican wave goes round the stadium,
Then the crowd lets out a roar,
Robinson runs over the line,
Then Robinson scores.

It's the last play of the game,
The ball gets kicked out,
The man of the match,
Is Robinson without a doubt.

Harry Bullock (13)
Rydon Community College, Pulborough

The White Horse

In its stable it stays,
And will occasionally give a neigh.

As the snow settles,
Covering up all the nettles,
When she gets turned out,
Galloping off,
She has no doubt,
She will just go and prance about!

In the morning when she wakes up,
She is covered in the snowy muck.

As she looks forward to the rest of the day,
Knowing she is safe, tucked up away,
And will occasionally give a neigh!

Emily Graysmark (12)
Rydon Community College, Pulborough

Money Box

On my window sill it lies,
Don't be daunted by its size,
My money box is full of cash,
Except I spend in a flash.

It takes me ages to fill it to the top,
But as soon as it's full the lid goes pop!

I can spend it here,
I can spend it there,
I can spend my money anywhere,
In and out the shops I fly,
If only I had more money for things I buy.

Eveé Bullock (12)
Rydon Community College, Pulborough

Bear

There once was a bear,
Hunting for prey,
Along came a hare,
There must be a way.

The bear approached,
As he got closer,
A huntsman was spotted,
A deadly bullet was fired,
Straight into the bear's chest.

The bear pleaded,
The hare fled,
The huntsman got what he needed,
'A nice woolly coat,' he said.

One day in the forest, the huntsman was there,
He turned around and saw a big bear,
After a gigantic roar,
The huntsman fell to the floor,
The huntsman was dead.

Tom Dunham (12)
Rydon Community College, Pulborough

The Flood Poem

The rain falls,
The river rises,
The fields flood,
It's full of surprises.

The trees fall,
They get washed away,
They hit the bridge,
Day by day.

Parents cry,
People die,
Houses flood,
Filled with mud.

Melanie Cave (12)
Rydon Community College, Pulborough

Loneliness

I am tired of crying, but I can't stop,
There is nowhere I can go,
Everywhere I go is darkness,
This loneliness makes you blue,
There is nothing you can do,
Only the things people can do for you,
But nobody cares for me,
It's always the simple things that hurt,
I want to know the meaning of happiness,
But will I ever?
The ones that care for are gone.

Alex Kwok (12)
Rydon Community College, Pulborough

Waves

In the middle of the deep blue sea,
The calmness of the waves are swishing by me,
I can hear mermaids whispering in my ear,
Telling me I'm delusional and should have no fear.

I can feel the sun burning on my skin,
The waves feel so cold lapping on my shin,
Where I go from here, I really don't know,
As everything around me is changing as I go.

I see no path, no way to shore,
Lost with no future, life has no story,
Books and tales are no good to me,
On a raft out at sea.

The sun is setting, the stars slowly appear,
This day is ending and my end is near,
Goodbye my friends, you are so dear,
If only now you would appear.

Waves upon waves came over me,
They carried me on a shore, you see,
Alone and alive I will survive,
I've learnt my lesson and now I'll strive,
To live my life and be satisfied.

Maria Paradise (12)
Rydon Community College, Pulborough

Just Fishing

Dragonflies over the water
Wind in the rushes
Canadian geese fly over
A water vole swimming
Ripples spreading
The cows want milking
A duck swims by
The dogs are barking
'Pass some bait Josh,'
A moorhen scuttling,
The smell of new hay
The sun in my eyes
Reflections of trees
My float dancing
It's gone under!
Is it a bite?
I strike the line
It's a big one
A two pound tench
Safely in the keep net
Time for my picnic
Ham sandwiches and cake
The sun on the water
Time for a nap
I like fishing!

Jonathan Harris (12)
Rydon Community College, Pulborough

Jersey

The Jersey cows are grazing,
The farmer ploughs the field,
No sheep or pig is in sight,
'Tis only cows that meet delight.

Waves crash down on Beauport Bay,
The sand is soft underfoot,
The rock climbing is made for sturdy feet,
Others it will only defeat.

The heathland has many a colour,
Deep greens, purples and yellows,
Against the sky and sea of blues,
This sight shall surely unsteady you.

So Jersey lives how Jersey is,
With many a view to see,
Like Jersey Zoo and the history too,
And going to visit the sea.

Phoebe Holland (12)
Rydon Community College, Pulborough

Imagination

All these mixed emotions,
Running through my head!
I imagine all my friends,
Waiting right up there!
As I make my way to them,
They give me such a glare!

I sit up in cloud nine,
I feel like it will all go just fine!
But all of a sudden, I wake,
I know it was all just fake!
I want to be back in my mind,
Where all the people are nice and kind.

Lauren Harthill (12)
Rydon Community College, Pulborough

The Tennis Tournament

The grass courts are ready,
My Wilson racket is steady,
1, 2, 3, bounces,
Throw - smash,
The ball is *Go!*
In the flashes of flashes,
The ball sails over the net.

However my opponent devastatingly returns the serve,
With a back hand slice down the line,
I reach,
I stretch,
It's no use,
The game's over,
My head was not in the game,
I was focusing on my problems at school,
I'm such a fool.

In the middle of the court, I'm shaking hands,
My head is down;
I'm embarrassed, humiliated,
And that's the tennis tournament for you.

Thomas Lavington (12)
Rydon Community College, Pulborough

The Secret Garden

T he plants swaying softly in the wind with sounds of whistling,
H ow the roses stand there so beautiful like a reflection in a
mirror of a lakeside,
E very vine crawling up the fence with lights shining
from every direction,

S un gleaming down on this magnificent garden with a
rainbow overhead,
E ven with the grass damp and vines,
C rawling everywhere, happiness surrounding the place
and peace emerged,
R ipe apples on a golden tree like a dappled roof with
a couple of fallen ones scattered wildly in the garden,
E ventually the sunflower reveals its inner colour of beauty,
T hen one downfall of rain and the sunflowers droop,

G oing very slowly the rainbow disappears gracefully
into the atmosphere,
A nd a dark cloud emerges with storms and lightning striking,
R ight in the heart of the secret garden,
D estroying everything . . . one year later,
E verything restored back to where it was, with the same
angle from the sun,
N ow it's all tidy again, a loving person has a bench there,
now everyone uses it, a relaxing place to think things out,
as it is a place for animals and people alike.

Dominique Burton (12)
Rydon Community College, Pulborough

Wolves And Deer

100 years ago, there was a forest in America,
Its name was Kebabo, in the north of Alexandra,
There were 4000 deer, and 4000 wolves,
The wolves preyed on the deer, and the people hated the wolves,
President Roosevelt wanted to protect the deer,
So he had to kill the wolves,
The hunters hunted 25 years, and there were no more wolves,
So the deer lived happily, inside their free kingdom,
They ate and ate, they grew and grew,
Within a few years there were over 100,000 deer in Kebabo,
But they were no longer happy,
There were no more greens in the forest so they ran out of food,
Then disaster struck,
The deer died of starvation and died of illness,
Within 2 years, there were only 40,000 deer left,
Within another 2 years, there were only 8,000 sick deer left,
Dying in Kebabo.
Roosevelt would never have thought: the wolves he killed
Were also the protectors of the forest!
The wolves ate the deer, so they kept the number of deer balanced,
And the wolves mainly ate sick deer,
Which stopped the disease from spreading,
The people would never have thought:
When they killed the 'Big bad wolf,' they killed the forest.

Frank Howell (12)
Rydon Community College, Pulborough

Libby

Libby's only 10 years of age,
But that doesn't stop her dad from his rage;
He drinks his beers from day to night,
He kicks and punches Libby with all his might,
Leaving Libby with a disturbing fright,
Her eyes fall with tears, the pain she feels,
She wouldn't be able to describe,
She wishes she weren't alive,
Libby always feels this pain every night,
She always sees this anger in her dad's eyes,
When he's been drinking.

Heidi Smith (12)
Rydon Community College, Pulborough

Sports Poem

Feet pattering on the ground,
People shouting, balls being passed,
Tackles take a crunch,
To the ground. Kick!
The ball flies over the posts!
The crowd roar as the player,
Celebrates the try.
The whistle blows as the drop kick
Goes up and then down,
Into a player's arms,
The final whistle goes as the rugby
World Cup Final ends,
20-17 to England.

Marcus Pringle (13)
Rydon Community College, Pulborough

Roller Coasters

Waiting, waiting,
In a long queue,
Just lining up for,
One small ride,
Well it's not really small,
In fact,
It's huge!
On we get,
OK, sit in seat,
And safety belt on,
Counting down until upward take-off,
Sweating hands,
Trembling body but,
Can't turn back now,
Uh-oh,
We're going up,
Don't look down,
Don't look down,
Looking down,
Oh help it's so high,
Well, here, we go,
Downwards,
Stomach lifted,
Heart in mouth,
I think I left my scream behind,
First three loops,
Coming up,
Legs hanging,
Eyes tightly shut,
Good that's over,

Oh no, second dip,
Hold on tight,
I think I'm slipping off,
Help me,
Hold on, hold on for dear life,
Hope that's the end,
Oh no, there's some sharp turns,
Bashing against the sides,
And another loop.
Oh great,
I am starting to feel a bit sick,
And here are some barrel rolls,
Ten to be precise,
I can feel all the blood,
Rushing to my head,
I'm going red,
I know it.
One last enormous dip,
Whoosh!
My hair is flying behind me,
And that's the end of the ride,
Belts off and out of the seat,
To the exit,
Thank goodness,
That's over,
But I might do it again,
Would you?

Emma Matthews (12)
Rydon Community College, Pulborough

The Sun

Isn't the sun the greatest thing?
It brightens our world and allows us to see.

It's strange to imagine our world without it,
No bird, no flowers or trees.

It would be like a gloomy dungeon,
Dark and quiet and cold.

There would be no movement, no sound, nothing.

No way of telling,
When night or day.

One thing's for sure,
We could never survive without it.

Harry Martin (12)
Rydon Community College, Pulborough

My Cat

His name is Trevor,
He's old,
He's clever.

He never has time to play,
Because he catnaps throughout the day.

He loves to eat,
And comes in from the garden with dirty feet.

He ran into the garden fence,
Because he has no common sense!

Vikki Longdon (12)
Rydon Community College, Pulborough

Dear Twister . . .

Dear Twister,

Why do you always rip up towns and leave homes in a wreck?

Why do you spin around like a washing machine on full spin?

Why leave people distraught and homeless?

Why do you come so quickly that you hardly give people

Time to evacuate or protect their homes?

You swirl and twirl across the country and overseas,
You pick up houses and topple over trees,
You hurt birds that chirp and snakes that hiss,
So why twister do you do all of this?

Hannah Wooster (12)
Rydon Community College, Pulborough

Day At The Zoo

The cheeky monkey hangs in the tree,
Making funny faces at me.

The parrot in his cage says, 'Pretty please,'
While all the mice nibble their cheese.

Koalas and zebras munch on the hay,
Making sure they have a good day.

Hippos wallow in the pool,
Just to keep themselves cool.

Lions and tigers love to roar,
While beautiful birds love to explore.

This is a typical day at the zoo,
Do you still think you can fill the keeper's shoes?

Tom Stiles (12)
Rydon Community College, Pulborough

The Windy Beast

The windy beast roars,
As it crushes the town,
Down the rains pour,
As the darkness comes around.

Demolishing everything,
That gets in its path,
Hiding, we wait,
For the mighty storm to pass.

Cars flying,
Trees knocked down,
But then, suddenly,
Calm comes around.

The war is over,
The damage is done,
But everything looks better,
From the barrel of a gun.

Houses flooded,
As they evacuate the town,
It should be two or three years,
Until our town is again found.

Ben Miller (12)
Rydon Community College, Pulborough

Lost And All Alone

Lost and all alone,
Did I choose to be like this?
Is it too much to ask for love, care and happiness?
No one there for me.

Lost and all alone,
Will I ever know what it feels like to have a family?
No one to talk to, no one to care for.

Orphanages, pain, suffer, horror, no one should go through it.

Jessica Leask (12)
Rydon Community College, Pulborough

Just Something From Me To You

Oh how did it get this way?
Things were meant to be different
All you had to do is say
I love you

I've been longing for you to tell me
But it seems as if the words don't exist
Now it seems that I'm in need
Of your love

Things were going fine
Up until this very moment
You were meant to be my boy
And I was meant to be your girl

I wish you still felt the same
As much as I do for you
Was this all just a game
Or do you still love me?

I guess it's the end
The end of you and me
There's nothing we can mend
Apart from your love for me.

Sherita Frimpong (14)
St Andrew's CE High School, Croydon

Trouble

If you could toss it out
Throw it past the moon
Be assured it won't
Come back any time soon

Would you believe that it had gone
That it would never return?
Realise what you are being taught
Take your time to learn

Or would you act
Like a lonely, spoilt brat
Pushing it all away
As if it's nothing more than that?

A simple event forgotten fast
A long and painful goodbye
A child who couldn't smile
Forcing out a single cry

An old and tarnished memory
I ask you what's the use
Of a single painful yell
Of an agonising abuse?

Miriam Rudge (15)
St Andrew's CE High School, Croydon

A Friend Like You

A friend like you
So hard to find
I searched for you everywhere
And now I found you
I am afraid to lose you

If you really love me
Deep inside
I am sure you will always be by my side

We will fight day and night
And together we will get through life
Your problems are my problems
You are hurt,
Then I am hurt too

Nothing in this world can put us apart
God had put us together
For the rest of our lives

Everywhere you go
I will always be by your side
I will forgive you for your mistakes
And I will be with you day and night

Friend like you
Bet no one has ever had
It is a blessing from God
That I hope it will last forever

Just want you to know
That you are the best friend ever
I will be by your side, no matter the weather

You and I will always be together
Nothing or no one can ever set us apart

And we will ride together to the very end
And be sure I will always love you the same way I did when I first
met you.

Denise Juvane (14)
St Andrew's CE High School, Croydon

People In Life

Babies, toddlers, children, teenagers, adults and elderly
all the people in life
but the main one that I think about is . .
Teenagers . . . my generation

People walking past
Cowering away just because of the way I look
I'm wearing my hoodie and
I'm avoided for my sense of dress

Then I take the hoodie off
It's like I took off my skin
People smile and stop avoiding me
Why, I only took off a jumper?

It's just not fair
I want to be treated equally
I am a nice person just
under a hood

So why?
Just treat me normally
I am just an average person.
What's changed when I put on my hoodie?

Please treat me fair,
just like you would want to be.
Please treat us fairly
for my generation.

Emily Cole (13)
St Andrew's CE High School, Croydon

My Poem About Teenagers

Teenagers, teenagers go to school
Teenagers, teenagers play football
Teenagers, teenagers all about
Teenagers, teenagers jump and shout!

Teenagers, teenagers play rugby
Teenagers, teenagers don't watch Teletubbies
Teenagers, teenagers wear bling, bling
Teenagers, teenagers praise and sing!

Teenagers, teenagers do a backflip
Teenagers, teenagers don't give me lip
Teenagers, teenagers bang on the door
Teenagers, teenagers break-dance on the floor!

Teenagers, teenagers jump around
Teenagers, teenagers touch the ground
Teenagers, teenagers everywhere
Teenagers, teenagers really don't care!

Kyle Henry (12)
St Andrew's CE High School, Croydon

My Generation

My generation is where I live,
Lots to have, even more to give.
My generation is full of kids
My generation is where I live

My generation is really fun
Lots to do for everyone
Everyone is number one
My generation is really fun

My generation is the place to go
In summer there's sun and in winter there's snow
My generation can really glow
My generation is the place to go.

Milly Smith (12)
St Richard's Catholic College, Bexhill-on-Sea

My Generation

Kids of today, they grow up fast,
Childhood play, games do not last,
So much to do, so much to see,
Hardly time to think about *me*.
Pressure for kids about exams and careers,
We have no time to think of our fears,
Homework and friends, good times and bad,
We run out of time, this is so sad.

World of today, can be very cruel,
Leaders fighting about who should rule,
Bombing and killing and evil around,
A glimmer of hope just needs to be found.
The world can unite in times of dismay,
Why does the world have to be this way?
We need to have a world with peace in our time,
To protect the future for us kids in our prime.

God of today, is a gift to us all,
Picking us up just as we fall,
He doesn't choose between colour or blame,
Just ask for help, call His name.
He helps us all in our times of doubt,
Our faith, His love is what it's about,
Our Lord, our Father in Heaven above,
We are his children all wrapped in his love.

Chloe Arnold (12)
St Richard's Catholic College, Bexhill-on-Sea

Everyone's Talking About . . .

Everyone's talking about the latest games,
But the latest games are all the same.

Everyone's talking about the latest news,
But I can get the latest news on channel two.

Everyone's talking about the latest clothes,
But I don't care when I wear from my head to my toes.

Everyone's talking about the latest tunes,
From February to February, from June to June.

Everyone's talking about the latest fads,
But sometimes they're just absolutely mad.

Everyone's talking about my generation
And my generation deserves celebration.

Louise Kimber (11)
St Richard's Catholic College, Bexhill-on-Sea

Modern Techno

Hi-tech transport games and sound.
iPods, micro chips, mega blasts pound.
Inventors are inventing and factories are making.
While the war in Iraq is still raging.

Smoke in the air.
Pollution in my hair.
Global warming everywhere.

Fighting and bombing and booming and screams.
Headlines on papers and new skinny jeans.

Celeb mags and gossip, CCTV
Is Big Brother watching me?

Plasmas DS Lites,
My generation has got it right!

Natasha Eames (11)
St Teresa's School, Dorking

To Love An Outcast

On one early time of the day,
I was wandering around the playground.
I turned and looked and there she was
Just sitting there on her own,
Without a thought of what other people think of her.

She is always alone.
Never has a partner for gym,
Always picked last for games.
She never interacts with the other children.
She just stalks the playground hunting for a friend.

She acts like an outcast
Even though she doesn't have to.
Everyone thinks she chooses to be alone,
But I know deep down in my heart,
No one wants to be alone.

Maybe she is shy,
Or maybe she just feels that she doesn't need a friend.
Maybe she is too consumed in her work to have a relationship.
She may feel love
But she may not understand it.

You see her staring
She is deep in thought,
Wishing to understand the true meaning of 'friend'.
Dreaming that one day someone will accept her for the way she is.
To treat her, to hug her, to love her.

She is an outcast
But she might not know it.
How does anyone know if they are one or not?
There is something that we can all do,
And that's to love.

Catriona Smitham (12)
St Teresa's School, Dorking

The Outsider

I am the outsider.
The different one.
My days are lonely
My nights are tearful,
My heart is empty
And my diary is blank.

I am a silent figure.
A quiet soul.
I am the shy one,
Unloved and abandoned by the world,,
Nobody talks to me
But everyone stares at me,
They laugh and mock my every action.

I am a single star.
Thrust upon the black, dark sky.
I am a discarded button
Detached from my comfort zone,
As the people trample on my feelings.
I am a sad kitten
Lost in a forest of hounds.

I am the outsider.
The different one.

Nikita Chaudhry (12)
St Teresa's School, Dorking

The Bakery

There's a little shop on the corner,
That always makes me smile,
I love every single bit of it,
Up to its old-fashioned tile.

As I stare in through the window,
Rain drips from the gutter,
It reminds me of early mornings,
And fresh baked bread and butter.

When I soon walk inside,
Warmth fills up my face,
It reminds me why the bakery
Is my favourite place.

I look at all the things,
That taste and smell so good,
Like cakes and pies and sticky buns,
It's my favourite type of food.

But then once more the time must come,
To choose what I must buy,
I finally decide upon
A lovely apple pie.

Ellen Mason (12)
St Teresa's School, Dorking

War

War is full of misery
It spread its icy fingers
Clutching at lonely hearts
It travels at speed
Leaving a trail of destruction
A heavy cloud of despair hangs
Above the heads of the unfortunate soldiers
War breathes sadness among the bereaved
It tears down communities
In a hungry rage
Leaving many to perish
And the survivors
To live on with a heavy heart
Never to be the same again
War is the reason this world is never at peace
It lives on to this day
It shows its ugly face at every opportunity
Seizing the vulnerable and the kind-hearted
Testing the strong one's strength
And although it may seem to have gone away
Somewhere in the world
While you read these words
War is raging.

Sarah Smith (12)
St Teresa's School, Dorking

Generation

PlayStatons kill me
TVs want to make me scream
Game Boys and Xboxes too
I don't mind computers
As I have loads of games I can play
They don't make so much noise

Cars are getting more expensive
And are polluting the air as well
Some people like showing off
And then do something silly
And end up in hospital
But I still love cars

There is so much gossip going on about celebrities
That I can't keep up
'Did you hear this
And did you hear that?'
Gets on your nerves sometimes
But you get used to it

TV programmes are making me go wild
Ugly Betty and The OC too
It's just the best
Sometimes I watch them day and night
That's the generation
Of 2007 for you!

Tertia Lynn (11)
St Teresa's School, Dorking

Generations

We now have Xboxes, PSPs, Nintendo Wiis,
and the most powerful things made
are a PlayStation3 and an Xbox 360.

We now have iPods, celebrity gossip and fashion
even mobile phones, digital cameras,
which you can take wherever you want.

We now have flatscreen TVs, Sky+ and much, much more,
far more channels than before.

We now have laptops, Internet shopping,
reality TV and satellite navigation.

We now have touchscreen phones
and swimming pools inside and out
and we can go to the other side of the world in just one flight.

Harriet Harman (11)
St Teresa's School, Dorking

My Generation

Born to a world of global warming,
Bad news coming, stormclouds forming.
The last generation, they had it so good,
They never thought about things they should.
Never had to worry about the sun's bad rays,
Never had to hide from the clouds' acid rains.
My generation has to turn it around,
It's up to us now to make everything sound.

Letitia Brien (11)
St Teresa's School, Dorking

My Generation

My gran was a child of the 1940s
My mum was a child of the 1960s
I am a child of the 1990s

My gran lived in WWII, the Blitz, rationing and Churchill
My mum lived with the Falklands, Northern Ireland and Thatcher
I live with wars in Iraq, fear of suicide bombers and Tony Blair

My gran travelled around on her bike and the bus
My mum travelled around in a very old banger
I travel around in a brand new silver Mercedes car

My gran played with dolls, wooden toys and card games
My mum played with Lego, Barbie dolls and board games
I play with PlayStations, Xboxes and computers games

My gran's teachers wrote on blackboards with chalk
My mum's teachers wrote on whiteboards with pens
My teachers use interactive boards with their fingers and pointers

My gran holidayed at Southport, Scarborough and Brighton
My mum holidayed through France, Holland and Spain
I have travelled the world to the USA, Africa and beyond

My gran had no television, video or DVD player
My mum had a black and white television with three channels
I have three TV screens, with 100 plus channels and a home cinema

My gran listened to rock 'n' roll on the radio
My mum listened to Showaddywaddy on her record player
I listen to greatest hits on my iPod

How things have changed!
How will things change?

Sinéad Nestor (11)
St Teresa's School, Dorking

Talking About My Generation

In two weeks I am going to Spain
And in eight weeks I am going to America
But if you couldn't do that, well, what a pain
Why don't we nip to Paris for the day
And catch the super fast Eurostar?
But if you go you would have to stay
EasyJet flights are amazingly cheap
You can travel all over Europe
But if you want to fly you would have to really dig deep
Mmm, shall we take the Lexus or the Mini
Or even the Saab for a spin?
But you only have one car, and it's teeny
We go via car or bus virtually everywhere
To shopping malls, the cinema and school
Whilst you walk because you cannot afford the fare . . .
For my birthday I want a new Nokia mobile phone
And the new iPod Nano Video in blue!
But if you want that, you'd probably have to take out a loan!
Why don't you come over and play on my Xbox
It will be so much fun playing my new game
But you prefer playing outside in the fresh air throwing rocks?
Tonight I'm going out to a concert with my aunt
And listening to all the cool music
But if you haven't got a decent radio . . . then I guess you just can't . . .
I can choose to eat out almost every day
Thai, Mexican, Indian and Lebanese
You would have to settle between fish and chips, or Chinese takeaway
But at least your can say you are fit and slim
Whilst we are all getting so obese
And yet so desperately wishing to be thin . . . !

Bryony Porter (11)
St Teresa's School, Dorking

My Generation

Mobile phones to keep in touch with your friends and families.
Take photos and sometimes go on the Internet.
If you have a mobile that does too!
iPods (Nanos) to get you interested in music.
Laptops so you can carry them easily instead of a computer!
Tamagotchis to play on and make friends.
Car/plane televisons to keep you interested.
Flatscreen TVs to make it look like you are at a cinema!
Remember to buy the popcorn!
Lots of new channels on TV for us to watch.
Sky+ HD so you have loads of different channels.
Nintendo DS to keep your children occupied.
Digital cameras so you can take loads of photos!
Digital watches to time or to tell you the time.
Computers to type up homework.

Lots of gadgets, all computerised,
Lots of things to do on them,
In my generation there are always things to do,
Go out with your friends and play,
Instead of playing with these elecronic devices
All day long!
You don't have to carry all these things around with you,
Just leave them at home and turn them off,
And enjoy the outside world,
Instead of being in the house all day long
Playing with these things.
Love the fresh air,
The sky and the sea,
Run with your dog if you have one
As you've always wanted to!

Natasha Rutherford (11)
St Teresa's School, Dorking

Talking About My Generation

A ll around the world bombs are being fired,
B ombs of destruction ruin everything,
O besity is in the headlines,
U niversal films are made showing
T rouble between countries.

M y generation is fun-loving and happy,
Y et all around there is sadness and fear.

G lobal warming is becoming a big threat,
E xtremes of temperature,
N ews of flooding and fires,
E veryone should be recycling, but are they?
R eligion is blamed for people fighting.
A nimals are dying from pollution.
T elevisions have hundreds of channels,
I Pod videos, music, there is noise all around us,
O zone layer is being damaged,
N intendo Wii is all people talk about.

Katie Tomkinson (11)
St Teresa's School, Dorking

Our World Today

Our world today is better than my mum's,
Full of new, better things.
Like iPods, phones and of course PSPs,
Nintendos, Sky+ and lots of DVDs.

But there are lots of other new things such as
The tsunami which killed hundreds of people.
There is also global warming,
This is killing animals and the world as you read this.

So I guess we are inventing electronics,
To replace all the animals we kill.
So I'm going to stick with my Game Boy for now,
And see what new things there are for the world tomorrow.

Angelina Wong (11)
St Teresa's School, Dorking

It's Happening . . .

It's happening now
It won't stop until we stop polluting the Earth
It's clearly a mistake we must have made
Now we recycle as much as we can
The government seems to plan to protect, but nothing much
                                        has happened as yet
As cars and lorries pollute the Earth driving around the planet like mad
What is it happening to us now?
Can we stop making mistakes?
It's happening now
It's called global warming

It's happening right now
As cars and buses suffocate the Earth
The invisible gases heat up the atmosphere
We try and use less
We cut down rainforests
And in every skinny tree, one by one,
We lose a bit of oxygen in every single one
How can we stop habitats from being extinct?
Why do we cut them down?
Global warming it's happening right now

It's still happening
The ice is melting fast
Soon the sea will flood and it shall be vast
Villages will disappear
As the sea creeps up on their farms
What shall we do then?
Rivers overflow and yet deserts will grow
I don't want these changes because the Earth is my home
What will become of my home?
It's still happening . . .

Lottie Smetham (11)
St Teresa's School, Dorking

My Generation

Lots of things have changed since our day
Here's what they are for me to say

Fashion is more important than it used to be
It's expensive and stylish and is great for me
Shops are good malls are great
Open on Sundays and open till late

Gadgets are fun and useful things
Laptops and mobiles with radical rings
New stuff is coming out every week
Just be aware I'm a total gadget freak

To travel it used to mean to go
To the nearest town or beach
But now we have trains and cars and fly
As far as planes can reach

At the end of this year I would have been abroad
Eight times to different places
Which makes my carbon footprint up to
Several million paces

Global warming is caused by the greenhouse effect
Walk or ride bikes or try to invent a transport with less
Carbon emissions to help to protect
We all need to reduce our carbon footprint
To help save the environment.

Jessica Bain (11)
St Teresa's School, Dorking

Some Things We Always Know

The world will keep on spinning,
No matter what I do,
No matter what I say,
To myself or to you.

My pen will keep on writing,
Until I let it stop,
Until the day I die,
If I want, or it drops.

My words will not be heard,
If I don't say them out loud.
I've got to say them clear
And show that I'm so proud.

I am me for a purpose,
But for what I am not sure.
I'm sure I'll find out soon,
Unless it was before.

There's two things that are certain,
In our world of today.
These are death and taxes,
At least that's what I say.

No two days will be the same,
Some good and others low.
Some things we can't escape,
Some things we always know.

Natalia Anderson (14)
St Teresa's School, Dorking

Generations

When my mum goes shopping she goes to her computer,
And presses lots of buttons to order things that suit her.
When Mum was small and went shopping with her mummy,
They went every day with small amounts of money,
No credit cards or supermarkets but friendly local shops,
A butcher, baker and a greengrocer who gave her lollipops.

The TV had only two channels when my mum was a baby.
But now we have lots, at least a hundred maybe.
You can have the radio on the TV now,
You can even rewind, pause the program you are watching.

iPods, Nintendos and PSPs are the new thing.
On Nintendo and PSP you can be king.
In the old days they didn't have anything like that,
One of the things in the old days is they could play with the cat.

Guns and terrorism are not as rare as they were years and years ago,
Nowadays terrorism happens nearly every day!
Loads of naughty people are carrying around guns, knives and bombs.
Lots of people are murdered every day
And the people that kill are normally mentally ill.

Jemima Hayes (11)
St Teresa's School, Dorking

Sport

I love sport, it's the best thing you can do,
Netball is the best and tennis too,
I would never stop doing my stuff,
There is never a point when I've had enough.
Taking part is what it's all about,
But winning is more important - there is no doubt
And when I do . . . I scream and shout,
We've been district champions in everything together,
Come on St T's we will win forever!

Alice Lines (14)
St Teresa's School, Dorking

My Generation

This century, number twenty-one,
There's newer versions of toys and guns.
There's different fashions, clothes and shoes,
And we have the Internet to tell us the news.

There's Internet shopping and mobile phones,
Celebrity gossip and fancier homes,
Digital cameras, theme parks or:
Sat Nav, laptops, flatscreens and more!

Lots of places now have TVs,
In aircrafts and cars, for you and me.
There's smart boards, PlayStations and way better jobs,
PSPs, USBs and bigger iPods!

Unfortunately, though, not everything's good,
There's more global warming in the world's neighbourhood,
Also terrorism and in some countries wars,
That's why now, there are more laws.

But still we've got all the latest things
And all the fun that they sometimes bring.
There's better CD players to play our favourite hits,
And Sky+ so you can rewind the best bits!

In our world, there's a birth every day,
A new little baby to grow up in its own way.
Another child in the family,
Just like we all used to be.

There's touch-screens and Nintendo Wiis,
Nintendo DS' and PS3s.
There's different watches like Baby Gs,
And prettier jewellery that you can see.

So that's the generation, century twenty-one,
Sit back and enjoy it, have some fun!

Amy Elizabeth Bates (11)
St Teresa's School, Dorking

Things I Really Care About

I love my family
The time we've spent together
My family has born and bred me
A family that sticks through thick and thin
And surrounds one another with sincere love and security
My mother who labours through love
Doing the endless chores of daily washing and cooking
My mother always prepares scrumptious meals
Which are eagerly devoured by the ravenous youngsters
My father who devotes all his spare time to his family
And labours through the work day
Extensive family whom we share close bonds with
And meet regularly at family occasions and leisurely get togethers
May we stay as close to each other as we are now.

Charlotte Groves (13)
St Teresa's School, Dorking

Seagull

One lonely seagull flies up high,
A magical sight flying the skies.

It sounds its voice and comes back down,
Swooping and soaring and lands on me now.

I feel its heat,
I feel its heart.

My hand reaches to show it the sea,
My hand extends to show that it is free.

Once again it is alone but not for long,
Soon it is joined and they sing a song.

They swoop and dive,
They will always survive.

Catherine Keey (13)
St Teresa's School, Dorking

Swimming - My Generation

There I am looking down at the deep blue, crystal clear H²O.
Ready to dive. The long and deep, far and wide.
My coach roaring to go, ready to start.

3, 2, 1 *go!* The blow of the harsh whistle, hits my ears.
Then I symmetrically hit the water.
I plunge down; then rise back up.

Head down, keep swimming, nearly there.
Look left, then right . . . oh no, I am losing . .
Keep kicking . . . nearly . . . I am there.

I have *won!*

Laura Emily Sessions (13)
St Teresa's School, Dorking

Singing Is My Joy

Singing is my joy,
A joy of life to me,
Singing on a happy day
Means a lot to me

Singing is my joy,
I sing all day and night,
Echoing up and down fields,
This makes me feel alright.

Singing is my joy,
I sing a song of wisdom,
I sing a song of words,
But all that I care about
Is that it can be heard.

Annabelle Ruddell (13)
St Teresa's School, Dorking

Sunsets At The Beach

Sand in my toes,
Wind in my hair
Midnight walks on the beach,
Living life without a care.

The sea on the horizon
Clouds in the sky
Waves splashing on the rocks
Watch the birds fly by.

The turtles crawling to sea,
The tide going out,
Crabs racing to their holes
Nothing about!

Fishing boats coming to port,
Dolphins gliding through the water
Sandcastles breaking
Hand in hand, like father
Like daughter.

Children going home,
Picking up shells
The whole place deserted
Sand stuck up your nails.

Not a drop of litter,
The sun begins to set,
So romantic
Another special day I won't forget!

I look out my window,
I stare and look mad
You ask me why I'm smiling
Then I explain what a brilliant day
I've had.

Francesca Layton (13)
St Teresa's School, Dorking

Talkin' 'Bout My Generation

Carries glinting kitchen sword,
And wearing finest Burberry cap,
Nike trackies we must applaud;
Stripes shining down his navy lap.

Acne spread like dotted jewels,
Across his fast-food face,
In a world where the burger rules,
And boozing counts as grace.

He signs his steady-handed mark,
The paint of reddest spray,
A master of this practised art,
Not one nice word astray.

Hoodie hunches overhead,
Past crisp, gelled, greasy hair,
Pearl-white trainers mark his tread,
Not his only sparkling pair.

His Strongbow like a trophy won,
For drinking under age,
From Unwins did he boldly run,
To his benchy bus stop stage.

Night approaches ever fast,
And lurks he in shadowed gap,
Surprising elder hobbling past,
For an off-peak happy slap.

Jessica Russell (13)
St Teresa's School, Dorking

My Mum

The most important thing to me
Are my friends and my family
But especially my mum
And she means lots to me.

Whenever I am upset,
She is always there for me,
She makes me smile,
And she looks after me.

She is very nice,
She is more than a best friend
She is always by my side,
Without her I don't know what I would do.

I love her lots and she makes me happy,
We have lots of fun together,
And we will love each other forever,
And ever.

She takes care of me,
And I feel very lucky,
To have a mum like mine,
As she is lovely and kind.

Emma Stack (13)
St Teresa's School, Dorking

My Family

M y source of happiness
Y awn is not the word to describe them.

F amiliar faces each time I wake
A lways supporting and protecting me
M e, there would be no me without them
I nteresting and always entertaining me
L oving, kind and what more would I say?
Y es! Lastly what would I, no you, be without your family?

Shemi Ibrahim (13)
St Teresa's School, Dorking

Fun In The 21st Century

DVDs
PSPs
I am not too hard to please!

Electronic games buzz and bleep
Swirling in my head, it's hard to sleep
So many things to do and play
So little time to sit quietly and lay.

Flights to all different places
Always packing my bags and cases.
Aren't we lucky to travel so much,
Great communication we're always in touch!

Mobile phones, iPods and more
Always chatting and laughing, friends galore.
Maybe my children will look back and say,
'Lucky old Mum, those were the days!'

Lucy Gavan (11)
St Teresa's School, Dorkingg37

If The World Was A Village

If the world was a village of 100 people . . .
82 would be non-white, and 18 would be white.
Why then is it the majority that are persecuted?

33 would be Christian, and 67 would be non-Christian
Why then are people of other religions persecuted?

5 US citizens would own 32 per cent of the world's wealth
Why then are people starving?

33 would be able to read, and 67 would be unable to read
Why then are they not taught?

50 would be malnourished, and 1 would be near death.
Why then are they not being fed?

This is my generation.

Aimee Church (13)
St Teresa's School, Dorking

My Generation

We've had the wacky hairstyles
The hippy-hippy clothes.
We've had the big hip stage
And the romantic era.
But now we are at my generation
It's better, in fact it's the best.

The World Wars have ended.
We have electric trains.
We have the London Imax
Museums for us all.
We have many restaurants
And scientists that know it all.

It is a hi-tech era
And in the future people will look back
At our plasmas, laptops and iPods
Our mobile phones, red, blue, silver and black.

In my era we have lots of food
Sweets, ice cream and cake
Chinese and Indian
Snails and slimy dates.

I love my generation.
I don't know what I would do without it.
I would be an evacuee and probably never see my real parents.
There are so many 'wicked' things in my generation
Bigger! Cool! It's the best!

But I think the best bit is my family and my friends.
My horrible brothers and sisters
My lovely kitty cat
My loving parents, Mum and Dad
And the neighbour's bat!

Rebecca Davidson (13)
St Teresa's School, Dorking

My Generation Poem

Girls of my age, what do we do?
We are not allowed a hullabaloo.
So what could we resort to
To stop us getting blue?

Music is good - I like my sound
It really helps my world go around.
While listening to the Arctic Monkeys
They will wipe away my frown
When all around is going down.

Fashion's a passion that's for sure,
The shops make sure that it's a lure.
That's the answer, the ultimate cure
To stop you feeling insecure
Buy these clothes and you will ensure
That you will look so very mature.

As a last resort when there's nothing to do
There's always TV to stop you feeling blue.
When there is no one to speak to
SpongeBob will see you through
Looking at life through his view.

When I get bored I play with my brother
Or if he's not there maybe my mother.
Sometimes it's hard to find another
Life is busy for every other.

So that's what it's like for my generation
It can at times feel a painful sensation.
It's hard to find relaxation
And sometimes it is all preoccupation
In the absence of congratulations
And this is all I've got to tell you.

Jasmin Van Den Berg (13)
St Teresa's School, Dorking

Tears

A baby is born,
The feeling of joy,
And here I am.

Baby's first steps,
The swelling of pride,
And here I am.

A toddler's words misunderstood,
The frustration builds,
And here I am.

The first bike ride,
The fall, the pain,
And here I am.

The school bell rings,
The excitement, the fear,
And here I am.

The ballet recital,
The nervous adrenaline,
And here I am.

The university beckons,
The sadness of goodbye,
And here I am.

The first pay cheque,
The excitement is overwhelming,
And here I am.

The wedding day,
Showers of happiness,
And here I am.

A baby is born,
The feeling of joy,
And here I am.

Tayla Coetzee (11)
St Teresa's School, Dorking

My Generation Thirty Years Ago!

Everyone has a mum and dad!
When we're teenagers we think they're bad!
Wagging fingers when homework's due
'Your bedroom's a mess, you can clean that too!'

'When I was a lad,' my dad often shouts
'*We weren't allowed to behave like louts*!'
We roll our eyes; oh this is a bore,
How many times have I heard this before!

When we sit down to watch TV
Mum rushes in, '*It's time for tea!*
When I was a girl we had to do our chores!'
We kids roll our eyes and think, *what bores!*

Thirty years later my kids sit down
I watch them and I start to frown
'It's time for tea - is your homework done?
Your bedroom needs cleaning. No time for fun!

Find my glasses! I can't see a thing,'
Suddenly I realise it has a familiar ring.
I sound like my mum, thirty years ago,
Nothing has changed, where did all the years go?

I look in the mirror and I look just the same,
As the picture of Mum that sits in the frame.
The wrinkles are familiar, all in the same place,
Thirty years have passed, I have the same face.

My husband comes home and shouts at our son,
'Leave the TV, get you homework done!'
My son looks up and I can see my dad,
I smile to myself, 'You're not that bad.'
In thirty years time, you'll be just the same,
As the picture of us that sits in the frame.

Felicity Woodward (11)
St Teresa's School, Dorking

What Is Important To Me?

In my life I believe many things.
It is important to me to have,
Friends, family, love,
It is important to have,
Morals, and not to have inconsiderate feelings.
It is important to be thoughtful,
Caring, sympathetic, trustworthy,
And not to be,
Heartless, cruel, selfish, rude,
Unjust, ill-natured.
It is important for everyone to help,
Poverty, the poor and ill
And not to help
The wrongdoing or to feed on others' misery.
It is important for me,
To get good grades,
And not to be,
Self-centred, malicious or violent,
It is important,
To encourage hard work and persistence
And not to encourage
Unfairness or dictatorship.
It is important to live,
In a caring society
And not in a merciless world.
This is what is important to me!

Sophie Vos (13)
St Teresa's School, Dorking

My Generation

Our clothes
Our make-up
Everything about us is different

But what about a long time ago
What did they wear?
What was their fashion?

We will not know
Was it cool?
Was it smart?

Did they always do their homework?
Were they goodie goodies
Or were they evil?

How about I ask my granny?
But what if she does not remember
I wish I was in her generation

I want to see what she would wear
Her personality
And if people liked her.

I know I can't be like her
I can only be me
The only person I can be is me

My generation
That's the only one I can be in
So this is my life, my happiness

This is me!

Georgina Hayes (11)
St Teresa's School, Dorking

I Love Mysteries

I love mysteries

Who is the culprit?
What is the theft?
Who is the victim?
What clues are left?

I love mysteries

Who has been murdered?
What has been stolen?
Was it silver?
Was it golden?

I love mysteries

Was it the maid?
Was it the mother?
Was it the nanny?
Was it the father?

I love mysteries

It was a theft
It was the maid
It was at poor Granny's
I'm afraid.

Francesca Cook (12)
St Teresa's School, Dorking

Moses My Cat

My name is Moses,
I get up every morning,
Stretch my legs and my body,
Let into the kitchen by my owner,
I claw the furniture.

My name is Moses,
I curl on the settee,
I am a lounge cat,
I clean my fur every day.

My name is Moses,
I graze my food every day.
Owners come back
I love them,
Sit on their lap.
I love them,
Stroke and snuggle.
I love them,
Chase birds and mice,
They're nice.

And that's my daily routine,
And that's my daily routine.

Ellen Jenne (11)
St Teresa's School, Dorking

The Whistling Wind

I am whistling, can you hear me?
I can see you but why can't you see me?
I am dancing, why won't you join me?
I am the wind whistling through the air
Come and join me and we can whistle together just you and me.
If in a rage, I can blow people's roofs off,
I can tear cities down.
But I can also make you laugh,
Can blow up the leaves,
Blow people's hats off.
I can tickle your cheeks
It's fun being the whistling wind
Why won't you join me?
I am whistling, can you hear me?
I can see you but why can't you see me?
I am dancing, why won't you join me?
I am the whistling wind, please listen to me
Please listen to me . . .
Please listen to me . . .

Beckie Barwood (11)
St Teresa's School, Dorking

What Bothers Me

What bothers me is global warming,
Gas, oil and coal burning,
Ice glaciers melting
And tons of scientists meddling.

What bothers me is rejection
People suffering from deception
People dying from hunger
And skies rumbling from thunder.

Some day I want to change this world
And make it a better place to live
With the help from all the people
It will become the best place to live.

Batool Siddiqui (12)
St Teresa's School, Dorking

Talkin' 'Bout My Generation

Now if I was to say
To somebody today
Tell me 'bout my generation.
They might reply:
Well, they lack concentration,
They don't eat any fruit,
And they don't eat any veg,
They have no discipline
And need a good kick in the shin,
The girls wear mini-skirts
And the boys - such jerks -
Wear their trousers right down low
They think it's so cool
When actually it's quite drool
To swear an awful lot.

And then I'd reply
In an outrageous tone:
It is very well-known
For an adult to have a good swear
And what to wear
Is totally our choice
As for what you put on
I don't want to comment.

Amy Clarke (12)
St Teresa's School, Dorking

Me And My Cardboard Box

I sit all alone in my cardboard box,
Under the bridge.

With only a blanket to keep me warm,
Even when it snows,
Even when it rains.

I do not work,
Relying on passers-by
To pop a penny in my hat.

Sometimes I am lonely,
With only the cold air as company,
My only comfort.

I sometimes wonder
What would it be like to be rich,
To have a home,
Or a family.

Why am I not accepted,
Into ordinary society?
Is it my looks,
Is it my clothes,
Or is it the fact that I have no money?

But until I become rich,
All I have to do is sit inside
My cardboard box.

Anna-Maria Mitchell (12)
St Teresa's School, Dorking

The Way Of The World

Because of what might happen
We play in the garden not the road.

Because of security
Big Brother sees our every move.

Because of expectations
We must do our best and get work done.

Because of great peer pressure
We must be 'cool' by acting uncool.

Because we expect so much
We feel so sad when we don't do well.

Because of electronics
We sit around and exercise less.

Because of processed foods
We don't eat five fruit and veg a day.

Because of medical science
We can survive illness and injury.

Because of our thoughts and feelings
We must put right what we know is wrong.

Because of our actions
We change the world we live in today.

Elena Mason (11)
St Teresa's School, Dorking

Our Generation

The shoe fashion for nowadays
is Ugg boots, pumps or flip-flops these days.
You wear long tops, pumps and leggings too -
I know this would be the fashion for you.

The electric technology nowadays
is camcorders and phones these days.
iPods and MP3s come too -
in any store - that's the store for you.

The environment nowadays
has been much better in quite a lot of ways:
less pollution, a new beginning, a main way of this is recycling.
if you leave the TV on standby then the tooth fairy will not drop by.

The climate nowadays has changed in quite a lot of ways:
the polar bears can't get back to their homes and the fish
                                        are frozen in big ice domes.

The summers are getting hotter
and soon England will be like Australia.

Rachel Gilbertson (11)
St Teresa's School, Dorking

The Autumn Mist

The morning sun unveils a picture
Through a car window is silken white
A swirling mixture
As we ascend and turn right
The sun gets stronger
The mist dissolves into pure light
As we gaze down below what was a valley
Is a hushed soft wrapping
We enter school with just a memory.

Bunty Rowbotham (13)
St Teresa's School, Dorking

Talkin' 'Bout My Generation

My generation is a
Funny old time!
From clothes to shoes to attitudes!

My generation is a
Funny old time!
We seem to like buggy eyes! (Oversized sunglasses)

My granny's generation is a
Funny old time!
They used to listen to the strangest music!

Everyone's generation is a
Funny old time!
There's grooves and moves and big bold lies.

Sabrina Beton (11)
St Teresa's School, Dorking

My Generation

iPods, TVs and computer games
That's the thing we do nowadays.

'High School Musical' is on TV
Everybody watches it, even me.

Sitting around watching TV
That has an effect on me.

The effect of TV is being lazy
When my parents were kids they were outside
                          smelling the daisies.

iPods that's what we like to listen to
Downloading songs that's what I do. How about you?

We can listen to music all day long
But is that really where we belong?

Sitting inside, is that where we're supposed to be
Or outside in the sunshine, running free.

Paige Prichard (12)
St Teresa's School, Dorking

Talking About My Generation

It's the age of mobile phones with cameras, games, even video,
With pets to wash and train on your DS Nintendo.

I hear my mother saying, 'No way!
We never used to have those in our day!'

A raspberry, a strawberry, a blackberry now we use,
So many gadgets and gismos our generation has to choose.

An iPod, well, they really are all the rage
For girls and boys, young and old, really any age.

But what about hopscotch, skipping, playing hide-and-seek,
What about going to the park? Bike rides once a week?

We wear Crocs, Celtic boots and short cropped tops.
Three quarter lengths. We love our shops lots.

Pink party limos are our ride to fun
We wouldn't even think about having a run.

Our music is funky, cool.
Our generation are no fools.

But are we really happy? I hear the oldies say.
Well as long as it's cake and ice cream for tea each day!

Francesca Summers (11)
St Teresa's School, Dorking

Shameful

As she bows her shameful head
The people turn and stare
Her squinted eyes, her broken nose
She hides behind her hair

As the children point and laugh
The adults also grin
What people think is mean and hard
Why can't they see within?

Her dowdy clothes are torn and wet
From ageing, time and rain
Still she can only stay alive
Through suffering and pain

Her last few crumbs go to the birds
They understand her best
Their little beaks peck hastily
Then fly off to the nest

She stands there firmly on the ground
She longs to be as free
Where no one laughs or jeers or points
Their words sting like a bee

The sun soon sets upon the park
The colours fade away
A stunning view, a peaceful sky
To end another day

She lies down like a mother cat
She stretches, has a yawn
The grass beneath is soft and dry
She sleeps there until dawn

She does not rise from her sweet sleep
Does not once move or stir
But has a smile upon her lips
An angel is with her

No more she bows her shameful head
But people's heads still turn
Harsh words can mean a lot to some
Can't people ever learn?

Hannah Edge (12)
St Teresa's School, Dorking

My Generation

TV, Nintendo DS and mobile phones,
That's what *my* generation's about,
Not yo-yos, paddle-balls or radios.

Footless tights, jeans and Ugg boots,
That's what *my* generation's about,
Not mini-skirts, rollerblades or stove pipes.

The Internet and iPods,
That's what *my* generation's about,
Not Pacman and black and white TVs.

The *Mir* space station,
That's what my generation's about,
Not a man on the moon.

Jasmine Brown (11)
St Teresa's School, Dorking

Outcast

Up the endless road he travels,
Blood-red in the setting sun.
Each step, agony beyond belief
Beneath his cut and bleeding feet.
A ragged shirt adorns his back
Covering the fresh scars from the lash
Of the slave master's whip.

His nut-brown face, lined and wrinkled,
Puckered up as silent tears roll
Down the hollow cheeks
All trace of defiance gone
Gnarled hands, worn with the labour
Of a lifetime's work grip a slender rod
Contrasting with the tired bent figure.

The sun beats mercilessly down
Providing no relief for the old man
Trudging wearily on.
Torment and shame writhe within him.
Cat calls and taunts ring in his head
Agony and misery clasp the bowed
Shoulders in a vice-like grip.

Up the road he travels
Nowhere to go, no friend in this
Bitter world who shut the door,
Block the bridge, so he cannot cross
Alone, deserted, friendless
An outcast.

Daisy Gilfillan (12)
St Teresa's School, Dorking

Outcast

Don't judge a book by its cover
That's what they all say until they see me
I may be

Black or white
Blonde or brown
Blue or green
Does it really matter?

Asian or Russian
Boy or girl
Tall or short
Does it really matter?

Young or old
Fat or thin
Rich or poor
Really does it matter?

Pretty or ugly
Clever or dumb
Common or posh
Does it really matter?

I wander alone
Looking for someone like me
Running away from children
Stone throwing, name-calling.

I am an outcast
Isolated from society
Pushed away from groups
A lonely life I lead.

Emma Robinson (12)
St Teresa's School, Dorking

The Outsider

The sand swishes against my polished shoes,
I am always alone and no one is ever with me.
All because of my dark mahogany skin
I am constantly left, neglected and destroyed.
Sometimes it gets aggressive and we quarrel,
They threaten me or try to blackmail me,
The worst of all is when they stop talking
And stare at me like a cat chasing a mouse
Or like a great white shark hunting a seal.

Everyone in the community is white,
I am black and have never belonged.
My parents have always been treated like dirt
And I have always been treated like rotten eggs.
They are as fierce as big hungry greyhounds
And as aggressive as parched Arctic snow wolves,
I am vulnerable and an easy target to hit.
There are lots of them, about 300 in school
But there will only ever be one of me.

The school students always ignore me
And the class teachers always stare,
They look at me like a scientist with a new species,
Like an animal to them that they find exciting
Because I am still not going to be one of them
And I never ever in my life will be
Unless this feud stops once and for all,
I will forever be left, neglected and destroyed,
Because there is only one of me and lots of them.

I have always been picked last for the team
And no one ever invites me to their parties
And they never ever stopped being mean.
I am like an innocent person that has been accused guilty,
I am always left out neglected and destroyed
For we all know we are different inside
Because the outside is not what counts,
They have still not learnt that,
I wonder if they ever will listen.

I am well and truly a black outcast
From the wealthy government as well,
My parents cannot vote in the elections
And we are not allowed successful jobs,
We cannot go to the private schools,
They have never ever allowed us
Even though my parents are rich,
We are left out, outcasts to our very own country,
My dad tried to stop them but they did not listen.

I try to be strong like my parents say, I try so hard.
No one is as courageous as my dad I know
And my skin tone has always been my weakness.
They hit me right where I am most sensitive.
I never was racist towards them
Yet still they treat me like an outsider.
Sometimes it gets so much worse,
They laugh, smirk and joke about it
And that is when I cry, so much.

They see me cry and they know it has worked,
That is when I am most vulnerable.
Anything they say hits me hard,
Stones crush my heart,
A sharp knife digs into my back.
That is when they have me,
Now I cannot ever escape.
Circumstances like that most often lead to suicide
Because there will only ever be one of me and lots of them.

Catherine Hopes (12)
St Teresa's School, Dorking

One Day I Was Kicked Out

One day I was kicked out,
I don't know how it came about.

All I am is different from the others,
But it gave me the right old shudders.

All alone, on my own,
Out of town, where I can't be shown.

Lots of feelings are buzzing around my head,
I am as cold and empty as a penguin that has not been fed.

People mistake me with what is on me,
But they never think for what is inside me.

Eight huge nobbly fingers on each hand,
So they say I could cover the land.

Every day I tried to blend in and please,
But the town still thought I had some sort of infectious disease.

That is the end of my tragic story,
I look for the end that it ends in glory!

Jessica Doherty (12)
St Teresa's School, Dorking

The Outcast

This character is very meek
She goes to protractor class every week
Her name is actually Agatha Teak
But everyone else calls her *the geek*.

She sits in a corner looking at files
Sitting there giving out geeky smiles
The maths teacher called her Agatha Teak
But everyone else calls her *the geek*.

She's so weird she loves homework
That's probably why she seems such a jerk
The science teacher calls her Agatha Teak
But everyone else calls her *the geek*.

She's rubbish at singing and dancing
Apparently she likes walking and prancing
The PE teacher calls her Agatha Teak
But everyone else calls her *the geek*.

Agatha Teak is really quite timid and shy
And hearing *'the geek'* it makes her cry
Her parents call her Agatha Teak
But everyone else calls her *the geek*.

Katy Kelly (12)
St Teresa's School, Dorking

This Is Me

As I dashed across the playground
Trying to escape the taunts that were being spat at me
I thought to myself, *am I really that bad*?

I am that weed in the shadow of the cherry blossom tree
I am 'that' kid who can't get up the stairs in school
I am the invisible one.

Looking at my wheelchair, cold as ice, clumsy like a drunken man,
Uncomfortable prison that has kept me back all these years.
The big rubber wheels that substitute my numb, lifeless legs that

Hang uselessly like rotting wood in a forest
From my twisted torso. Why do they talk loudly to me?
People don't seem to realise that I'm not deaf as well,

It's only my legs that don't work.
Why don't people see me, my chair is only just out of sight line.
Why am I the target of bullies, I have a heart as well.

I can still get to the end; I just go about it the different way,
I am strong, stronger than most people, I get through the humiliation
And ridicule of the others who think they are better than me.

I know I am different but not that dissimilar
I may look and act unusually on the outside
But on the inside I am just the same as every other person.

I am who I am and no one can change me
All they can do is see me in my true form
A child like every other, not an *outcast.*

Eloise Smith (13)
St Teresa's School, Dorking

Leave

He runs, he jumps, he tries to hide
They sprint, they shout, they shake inside.
The loud thud of hooves, the soft pad of feet
The angry people, they race up the street.

As scared as a small child lost in the park
He keeps on through forest dark.
But what will he do? He does not know
All he knows is that he has to go.

The people stop running and look around
They sprinted, they shouted and now he's not found.
They get to their homes and quietly regret
Why aren't they happy? That's what they don't get.

They feel like barbarians that chase him away
Why weren't they kind, why couldn't he stay?
He wasn't like them, for that they were scared
To take him in? They weren't prepared.

His long, dark shadow disappears
The moment unlocks his deepest fears.
Crouched deep in the woods he lets out a cry,
He moans as he watches the people go by.

Isabel Nicholson Thomas (12)
St Teresa's School, Dorking

The Thing

He is not wanted, he is alone
He is like rubbish on the beach
that no one wants to touch

He makes sounds like an injured beast
He scares all those that he sees
He smells like rotten meat
and looks as if he will kill

He does not care for much at all
and shows his anger like a raging storm
He will curse for he is an evil spirit
You should stay away

Is he man or is he beast?
Is he flesh and blood?
What is it that we fear
Just like our worst nightmare?

Be careful,
For what you dream may come true!

Hannah Paul (12)
St Teresa's School, Dorking

The Teacher's Pet

Mondays, Tuesdays,
Wednesdays, Thursdays
And Fridays will always be bad;
They'll taunt me forever,
My 'friends' are terrors
Just because I'm the teacher's pet.

I weep and I whimper,
To my stepmother every day
She murmurs, 'Oh well . . .'
But she really is laughing
At my sadness and sorrow.

I live my life like a passer-by
Forgotten like a lost memory;
My life as a loner
Mistreated by my 'owner'
What's the point of living if you're me . . .

Lara Heus (13)
St Teresa's School, Dorking

The Tramp

Alone every single day
I've never known another way
No one there to help me when things are bad
All great things to me look sad

Life in a box really ain't that great
Oh, wouldn't I just love a meal on a plate
Selling magazines on the street
Oh, wouldn't I just love to be neat

I wake up in the morning
And smell like a pile of dirty laundry
People turn away in disgust
And only look at me if they must

Dirt encrusted on my nails
Clothes torn, hair matted
Begging for money on a train
People muttering that I'm a pain

Life is tough on the road
And, guys, I just wanted you to know
My life is a heavy load
Of memories I wouldn't want to share.

Fiona Graham (12)
St Teresa's School, Dorking

The Outcast

An outcast is forgotten,
And pushed away,
By people who are rotten,
Every day

An outcast is alone,
Because no one wants to play,
Because an outcast is prone,
To ruin their day

An 'it' person is forgetting,
And pushing away,
And is being rotten,
Every day

A caring person is trying,
To encourage play,
Without prying,
And ruining the day

An outcast is not,
Because hate is at bay,
Because care cares a lot,
Every day.

Amilia Bishop (12)
St Teresa's School, Dorking

Tramp

He lies in a heap
outside the super mart
though his cup begs for money
his eyes beg for sleep

Toothily he grins at the ladies
spits at commuters
laughs with the men
and coos at the babies

With tongues of flint
the children cry
taunt and whisper
chide and hint

His breath reeks of gin
as he coughs long and dry
he sleeps now never to wake
from his smelly old bin.

Sarah Scott (12)
St Teresa's School, Dorking

Why?

Why is the world so horrible, full of evil times and people?
Why is my life so thought of, because in the end it's nothing?
Why are so many people dying, because people are
                                        so self-absorbed?
Why am I here? What is the point of this?
Why do so many people worry about what will happen?
Why do people live in the past if it doesn't matter?
Why do people insist on being the best if someone's just going
                                        to be better?
Why if so many things are happening does no one write it down?
What is the point of life? It doesn't matter it's going to end!
Why don't I care that I and everyone I know will die and be forgotten?
It is because we are and were and we will be remembered but not
                                        will be.

James Beaton (13)
Seaford College, Petworth

Icy Mountain

I'm on an icy mountain high in the sky,
I'm twisting and turning all through the restless night.

And now I find I'm starting to fly,
I'm giving myself a humungous fright.

Now I've landed on a silky soft cloud,
I finally sit up and open my tired eyes.

Some people are screaming ridiculously loud,
I look around to see where my bedroom lies.

My eardrums are burning as I see the forbidden daughters,
I'm awake and hugging my bright yellow ted.

I fall off the cloud and land in the murky waters,
But really I've only fallen out of my cosy bed.

These changes I realise are very vast,
From the real world to the surreal world,.
Is where nothing much lasts.

Chloe Fallows (12)
Surbiton High School, Kingston upon Thames

Dream . . .

The heat is sweltering,
My feet feel like hot coals are on them,
I'm wearing a gold crown
And white linen.

Someone calls my name
I travel to the voice
And find a king
Sitting with servants around him.

He has a present for me
I search and find
In front of me
A beautiful white stallion.

Sophie H Hughes (12)
Surbiton High School, Kingston upon Thames

Dreams

Dreams are your imagination,
Your thoughts,
They're timeless.
Dreams are like a golden peeling,
Lettering around you.
Dreams are timeless, your inspiration.
Dreams are exotic,
Crimson with blood and amber eyes.
Dreams are good and bad thoughts,
Family and friends,
Your inner you.
Dreams are thick armour surrounding you, surreal,
They're elemental and strange.
Dreams are different and infectious feelings.
The clock strikes all is lost,
In your own little world.

Shania N Matthews (12)
Surbiton High School, Kingston upon Thames

The Mirror!

I look into the mirror,
And in its face I see,
A beautiful girl,
I see me.

This mirror tells the truth,
The beauty of what's inside.
Of every single person
And all shall abide.

Josie Gebbie (13)
Surbiton High School, Kingston upon Thames

Nightmare Poem

Her hair was as dark as the night sky above
Her wart as big and fat as a pig after eating
She wore a long scarlet-red robe that twinkled in the night on its own
We came barging through as we ran down the hallway
We were forced here, had to do chores
You have to do the chores or else you will get beaten
Rotten teeth like the apples you have for about a year disintegrating
But we can't leave
She won't let us
(Ring ring)
The sound of my alarm clock at last.

Emma Vartevanian (12)
Surbiton High School, Kingston upon Thames

In My Subconscious

I'm spinning
Round and round,
I'm flying
Still spinning
Above clouds,
I'm falling
Down and down,
I'm bouncing
Still spinning
High in the sky,
I'm laughing
Ha, ha, ha,
I'm sitting
Still spinning
Floating,
And it's black
Black and white,
I'm a wet pink shoe!
Help!

Annie Sibthorp (12)
Surbiton High School, Kingston upon Thames

Down The Little Garden Steps

She stepped down the little garden steps,
counting each one as she went,
she saw in front of her a gate,
with ivy wrapped around it,
she put her hand on the gate
and pushed it forwards,
she stepped out onto the path,
which led through the garden,
she walked along, breathing in the fresh air,
looking at all the flowers around her,
she could see a box in front of her,
it was tiny with hinges of gold,
she knelt down to pick it up,
inside was a gift, a ring,
she stood up straight, observing the ring,
it was gold, just plain gold,
she could see a figure emerging from the mist,
he was walking towards her,
she could now see his face and what he was wearing,
old-fashioned clothes, he had long hair and an earring,
she looked at him wondering who this strange man was,
he spoke to her, he said he was writing a play,
she was in it, she was the main part,
he gave her a gift, it was a ring,
she realised that the ring she found was not for her,
it was for the play that she was in,
she looked at the ring the man had given her,
it was also gold, but with three diamonds on,
she took it and said, 'Thank you,'
the man said, 'I will see you soon,' and just left,
she watched him go and then walked the other way,
back down the path, through the gate, and up the stairs.

Ellie Mallen (1)
Surbiton High School, Kingston upon Thames

Towering Over Me

It was there,
Towering over me.
The church
Why am I here?

Everything was completely colourless
But I didn't notice.
I lived in a lifeless world
Without noticing!

We walked into the chapel
But before I took a step in I heard a hoot behind me
A smoking beast chugged along
I wanted to look away but I couldn't tear my eyes away

It was calling me
I had to respond
I jumped
I was hurtling down the tracks on the front of this train

A girl was there
She materialised out of nowhere
Smiling and chatting but about nothing
She had evil in her eyes

She pushed
I fell
A scream as I saw the ground
A twisted laugh
Silence

I woke up
I went downstairs to watch TV
Why?
I never watch TV in the morning

I pressed the button and it jolted to life
A once dull object with a dark screen now showed a picture of my face
I was falling!
I screamed and finally woke from my slumber.

Eloise Moench (11)
Surbiton High School, Kingston upon Thames

Running Tears

The clock strikes
Covered in not blood but tears,
Pale grey the colour of mist,
There is golden lettering,
Dizzy with heat,
And shuddering,
I screamed a cry of shock,
Panting with every step,
All is broken,
A black speck in a wall of light,
I am lured to its lair.

Abigail Croft (12)
Surbiton High School, Kingston upon Thames

My Dream, The Poem

Aeroplane,
Crash,
Icy cold sea,
Titanic,
Saved,
Icebergs,
Crash,
Thick white snow.
British Airways sign staring up,
Family and friends, gone,
Half frozen,
Teddy bear,
Dead.

Susanna Bird (12)
Surbiton High School, Kingston upon Thames

The Enchanted Garden

Today I found myself somewhere enchanted.
As I walked through an arched door,
White doves flew around me.
I had entered a magical garden.

There were exotic flowers and plants everywhere.
Lilies, orchids, fuchsias and many more.
All different colours, they looked supernatural.

Butterflies fluttered in and out of the plants,
I could hear birds singing in the distance.
Little fairies were dancing on the flower beds.
It was all very surreal, yet mysterious.

I found myself walking to a small stream,
Which trickled down small cracks in the garden.
Then just by the steam on a paving stone,
Was a rectangular silver container,
I opened it to find a single white rose . . .

Charlotte Coleman (13)
Surbiton High School, Kingston upon Thames

Freeze

Mysterious whispers inside my head,
Feeling a cold chill down my spine,
I wander hopelessly around the room,
A haunting touch in every corner,

A cold voice spoke,
I span around
And he stood there,
The man who lurked in my dreams . . .

Melina Schoenenberger (11)
Surbiton High School, Kingston upon Thames

My Visualisation

I walked down the stairs
Completely full of air.
I thought I was just floating
I also thought I was going to sink
Right through to the bottom of the ground.

I reached the bottom of the stairs
And stepped outside to be granted
By a beautiful rose flower.
Next to it was a daffodil.
They smelt of violet sherbet sweets.

I walked through the hedge path
and I thought I saw Shakespeare.
I was sure my eyes saw wrong,
his silky blond hair and his blue eyes made him so real.

I ran to my image I thought I saw
and I came close and it was real.
He gave me a circular present.
I wondered what it was.

He also got a gift too, from me.
I opened my gift, it was a picture.
I gave him a picture of me.
He also gave me a script.
Completely based on me.

Mathilda Lucas-Box (13)
Surbiton High School, Kingston upon Thames

Feather - Haikus

He gave me a ring
It was silver in colour
With Shakespeare engraved.

I gave him a box
Inside it was a feather
A white, soft feather.

Rosie McGurk (14)
Surbiton High School, Kingston upon Thames

Shakespeare's Dream

My head full of ideas,
Bursting with plays,
Popping with novels,
Maybe a lover's tale gone wrong,
Or a tragic ending.
Why won't it make sense?

It's hard to concentrate,
With all my ideas,
So difficult to study,
I just want a moment by myself,
When I can't hear the drumming.
Why won't it make sense?

I want to write all of them down,
But I don't have enough paper,
I try to merge my ideas together,
Why can't it all make sense?

Hettie Taylor (12)
Surbiton High School, Kingston upon Thames

I Am What I Am

I am water flowing along a stream
I am green grass in a secret garden
I am a tortoise exploring my jungle
I am air floating in the sky
I am a heart beating very fast
I am sunny with some clouds around
I dream that I am on a beach developing a tan.

Florence Green (11)
Surbiton High School, Kingston upon Thames

Who Am I?

I am a huge bouncy castle,
I can hold lots of friends and will try not to pop.
I am a loud chatterbox parrot,
I am colourful and once I talk I can't stop.

I am as bright as orange,
I am there to give everyone a smile.
I am like a sunny day,
My radiant rays can travel for a mile.

I am like a star,
I am sharp in some places but I'm also fun.
I am like fire,
Roaring and raging yet as bright as the sun!

Emily Steer (11)
Surbiton High School, Kingston upon Thames

I Looked

I looked into the distance seeing,
Flowers of red and purple,
Seeing people dancing,
Looking happy,
It was a carnival of colours.

I was peaceful, no fighting,
No war,
I see a big stage,
People acting my play,
It was great.

It was all my work over the years,
Being acted, it was magical,
My wish had been granted,
I felt a whirlwind of emotions,
But happiness came out on top.

Kathryn Cleaver (12)
Surbiton High School, Kingston upon Thames

Hermia

As I was wandering in the wood one day
I came across a young maiden.
She sobbed to me:
'Oh please, young sir,
Help me out for I am lost
And my lover has left me.
It was only yesterday I was in the
Hearts of two,
And today in the hearts of none.
Oh, dear young sir, please
Help me understand why are
My friends being wicked to me,
What have I done wrong?'
I said to the girl:
'Don't fret, young maiden,
I am sure you have made a mistake.
Was your true love true to you?'
'Yes,' she replied.
'Then I am sure you are mistaken,
For true love does not change that quickly.
Before the day is finished
He will surely love you again.'

Nayantara Preston (11)
Surbiton High School, Kingston upon Thames

Dreams

Thick armour of green slime,
Slug like bodies,
Rocking truck like waves in a sea,
Eyes wide open staring straight at us,
Driving to Mexico in an awkward position.
I was dead, nothing could be seen.

Melina Amin (12)
Surbiton High School, Kingston upon Thames

I Am . . .

I am a butterfly about to spread my wings
Ready to see the whole wide world!

I am a fluorescent pink - glamorous
And cheerful!

I am a cat - elegant, adventurous, and loves food!

I am water - pure and flowing!

I am a star - always ready to turn the next corner!

I am the sun - sparkling and bright!

I am a happy dream - ready to awake someone with a smile!

Brodie Prowse (112)
Surbiton High School, Kingston upon Thames

Untitled

Oh beautiful Titiana
So proud to be the Queen
But what she dreams of
Is from my quill to scene

Gossamer wings silky and clear
Glistening in the glowing moonlight
Nature cloaks her locks of gold
And keeps her hidden from our sight

As she lies there slumbering deeply
In her leafy bed
I scribe for her a destiny
That King Oberon has said

Fateful purple nectar
To your lids apply
What fortunate creature on your love
Can now rely?

Grace Miller (11)
Surbiton High School, Kingston upon Thames

Depths Of A Shadowy Forest

In the depths of a shadowy forest,
In the morning's early hours,
I stumbled upon an arrogant fellow,
Full of proud and superior speech.
'Hey sire,' he called,
'Come act in my play,
Cast your eyes on my script,
Examine the words that I wish you to utter.'
'Alas dear friend,
Speak you no more.'
I declared to his deep disappointment.
'The play it is mine, it comes from *my* mind,
And you are a character in it.
You have jumped off the page, and are hard to control!
Bottom, you ignorant beast!'
As I turned away I regretted the time,
I created the ass-headed fellow!

Tamara Mulley (11)
Surbiton High School, Kingston upon Thames

Mocking Me

Everything went as *black* as night,
A grinning smile floated towards me,
Mocking me,
A flash of blinding light,
A thumping noise like a herd of elephants,
A thick oozing liquid ran down my back,
My head whacked on a rock as I was dropped,
Lush green grass beneath me,
Sparkly wings spurted from my shoulder blades,
Another flash of light,
Silence.

Bethan Baxter (12)
Surbiton High School, Kingston upon Thames

Terrified To My Bones!

I walk through grey nothingness,
With no happiness,
I see something,
An angry beast.

It has scarlet-red blood,
Dripping from its fangs,
Its hair is static,
Was running like it was frantic.

Stares with its black beady eyes,
Makes me dizzy in the head,
Terrified to my bones,
Run through the pine green leaves,
And step on grey cobbled stones.

Antonia Adams (12)
Surbiton High School, Kingston upon Thames

All But One

I close my eyes in reality,
Darkness . . . nothingness . . . light!
Firelight,
Blazing, scorching, burning.
A bridge of destiny.
A family of anxiety one side,
A frightened girl, the other.
A step of fortune,
Then another . . . without.
The bridge is falling, tumbling,
All but one plank.
She hangs on,
Jumps,
And caught!

Josie Chamberlain (12)
Surbiton High School, Kingston upon Thames

Shakespeare And Me

The stairs I walked down were old and steep.
I ended up in a room with a bucket and mop.
I stepped outside, into a beautiful garden.

I walked along a path with grass both sides.
I found a box with money inside.
I then saw a figure emerging ahead.

Shakespeare.
He asked me if I would like to be in his play.
He then handed me a gift.

I then walked back along the path.
Found myself in a room with a bucket and mop.
Walked up the old, steep stairs.

Where was I?

Grace Martin (13)
Surbiton High School, Kingston upon Thames

Who I Am

I am a wall as thick as could be
I am blue like the sky on a summer's day
I am a cat prowling around on a cold winter's night
I am air
I am a circle rolling around a bright sunny garden
I am hail slamming down on a shed roof
I dream of my cat.

Hannah Wood (11)
Surbiton High School, Kingston upon Thames

Meeting Shakespeare

I walked into the garden
And sat down on the bench.
I could see the deep red rose,
I could smell the freshly cut grass,
I could hear the swishing soothing sound of the willow tree
And I thought what a wonderful thing nature is.

Everything around me was perfect.
Everything was in place
Except one thing was different,
One thing should have not been where it was then.
A present lay neatly wrapped on the lawn.
It was a black box with a ribbon and a bow.
Somehow, yet I am unable to explain why, I knew a biro was in it.
Suddenly I was distracted as a distant figure approached me.

A ruff was worn around his neck and a cloak trailed behind him
and then I knew that this person was none other than Shakespeare.

Suddenly I knew who the present was for.
Shakespeare sat down beside me and said, 'Hello.'
I was taken aback but I nodded my head.

Shakespeare said he had a present for me.
Instead he sat and thought.
Shakespeare thought for a very long time,
And eventually said that he would give me the gift of rhyme!

I gave him the biro so out goes the quill,
No more blotting the paper, no more ink to spill.
He told me to practise rhyming because I was to be in a play,
A play about a girl who met Shakespeare, one fine day.

Amanda Stafford (13)
Surbiton High School, Kingston upon Thames

My Meeting With Shakespeare

There I was, at the top of the green carpeted winding stairway,
Looking down 10 steps which drifted off into the distance,
I climbed down them, counting every step I took,
At the bottom, I reached a small path which I followed,
Eager to explore, I entered a huge round garden,
Outlined with beautiful, bright flowers.

Then I heard a voice calling out for me,
I turned my head to see who it was,
There stood a man, looking up at me,
In black tights, a gold hoop earring and a ruff around his neck,
Immediately I knew it was Shakespeare.

After we had greeted each other, he told me of his new play,
Informing me I was the main character of his new invention,
My eyes grew wider as he explained my role,
Excited to be in company of such an incredible man.

It soon came the time when I had to depart,
But before I left, he gave a silver medallion,
Decorated with diamonds,
He placed it in my hand and told me I would need it in the near future.
However, before I could question, he disappeared into thin air,
Just like that.

Zoe Hill (13)
Surbiton High School, Kingston upon Thames

The Poem Of My Dream

It was only ten steps,
Ten steps to enter.
As my hand slid down the brown oak bannister
I entered a beautiful decorated room.
The walls were beige with beautiful gold flowers carefully painted on
And the floors were a matching brown oak to the bannister.
Despite the vast amount of decoration, there was nothing in the room,
Nothing more than great long walls.
Except, I could see right to the end of this over-sized room
Where two glass doors opened onto what seemed to be a garden.
I quickly walked down the room, eager to see what I might discover.
To my delight I saw an endless meadow with green grass swaying
Gently in the warm breeze.
A gravel path meandered through the meadow, which disappeared
Over a hill in the distance.
I skipped down the path with the sun shining on my face.
I made an abrupt stop to discover a small plastic container
With a fuchsia-pink bow around it.
I picked it up, undid the bow and opened the lid.
In the container I found a little gold key.
Suddenly I looked up and saw a man coming over the hill.
He looked like he was coming this way and with every step
He got closer.
Before I realised the man was about twenty metres away,
And that was when I could just make out who it was.
Much to my amazement it was the poet and playwright Shakespeare.
William Shakespeare.
He was wearing what seemed to be a 16th century outfit,
With a collar around his neck.
He had a moustache and an earring in his left ear.
Then he spoke about writing a play with me in it.
I replied, asking him what about.
He did not reply, but instead gave me a small gold locket
With a picture of my family inside.

He told me that the play had something to do with the locket.
I then handed him the key and he thanked me, as if knowing
What it was about.
Shortly after he left, and went in the opposite direction from
Which he came.
I too left, and went back down the path, and through the long room.
I returned to the ten steps and walked back up them.

Annabel Harris (13)
Surbiton High School, Kingston upon Thames

Dark Dream

In the forest, surrounded by leaves
Lost in a plethora of trees
Surrounded by surreal colours, flashing rapidly
Spiders crawling underfoot
Slimy moss stuck to rotting logs

All is quiet
Croaking crickets
Leaves brushing in the wind
Sudden screams
Wings flapping in the air
Mud squelching by your feet

People misjudging
Scary moments
Disbelief between lovers
Disaster strikes
Confusion leads to chaos.

Jessica Heyward-Chaplin (12)
Surbiton High School, Kingston upon Thames

No Life To Be Seen

There was no life to be seen,
No movements,
No noises,
No birds singing,
No ants crawling,
No snakes hissing,
No dolphins splashing,
Nothing,
Red planet, deserted.

In the silence,
Rustling,
Cracking of twigs,
Deep in the trees,
Darkness shadowing them,
Sheltering them,
Lay a family,
Curled up together,
Their long soft ears drooping from 10 little
Soft, sweet faces,
Puppies.

There were other noises,
Other creatures in the trees,
There was crashing,
Trees fell in the distance,
Machines ripped trees from the ground,
The family fled,
Scattered into many directions,
Caught in nets,
Taken away.

Years passed,
The family,
Reunited once more,
Only 6 young terriers,
Homeless, alone,
Abandoned,
No parents,
No friends,
Deserted on the forest floor,
Food surrounding them,
They did not know where to look,
There was no longer such a family.

Fenella Boulter (12)
Surbiton High School, Kingston upon Thames

My Visualisation

I walked among the smiling daisies.
Sunflowers beaming in my direction.

Lazy bees droned among the wallflowers.
A light breeze tickled the leaves.

Scents of lavender and rosemary fused in the summer air.
The heady smell or ripe grapes rose dizzyingly from the vines.

The husky croak of a frog,
Echoed round the leafy pond.

There on the ground lay a silver box,
Sunbeams dancing on its shiny blue bow.

Here was my gift for the great man himself.
Would Shakespeare come to the garden that day?

A willow tree parted and there he stood,
His crisp white shirt fluttering in the breeze.

'Ah, a quill!' he said, as he picked up my gift,
And stared at the pen like a holy relic.

Lucy Purslow (13)
Surbiton High School, Kingston upon Thames

Heart Of Silver

I gently walked on the glistening green grass,
Closely admiring the brilliant red daisies,
The towering maze of hedges on either side ensnared me in my
Own prison,
The entwining vine of roses like hope on a dark day.
Enchanting flowers were accompanied by exotic plants,
But it was not these that enthralled me,
For the company of the colourful butterflies and singing birds
Kept this exquisite world alive.

A twisted stone path led me to the hallowed haven of water.
Sunshine danced on this divine pool of clear blue,
While I cautiously stepped on the stones that floated,
My eyes fell on a silver body drifting on the water like a cloud
Swimming in the air.
A radiant boat that comprised a gift,
Half a silver locket in the shape of a heart,
Encrusted with diamonds and an etching in a language not known.
It was a gift that did not belong to me,
But had to be delivered to the rightful owner.

I continued my journey through this world of unseen pleasure
And saw the man I had been waiting for.
A yellow and purple striped coat and radiant blue trousers
Dotted with red!
It was the sight of him that struck me most.
He tells me he is here for a purpose,
To write a tragedy about me says Shakespeare,
With secrets untold and mysteries unveiled.
'What is it about?' I ask him,
But I get no reply in return.
'You are the only person who must not know,'
Confused, baffled and perplexed.

He hands me a silver circular box overflowing with surprises
And mystery
Curiosity opens it and finds half a silver locket.
Half a silver locket in the shape of a heart,
Encrusted with diamonds and an etching in a language not known.
'Take it to the place it belongs,' I am told.
I realise then why I had been given the gift
I join the two halves.
The job is done.

We are about to go our separate ways
'Farewell my dear, but we shall meet again,' says he
I turn to depart and walk back
The sun is hiding, the moon is asleep
The mist is my only companion through the gloom
The pond is black, the boat has departed
I see no flowers, I see no life
Death and darkness prevails.
The wilted flowers and dry grass create misery in the prison
Of bereavement.
The birds are gone, the butterflies missing
And yet, the roses live on.

Ravleen Kaur (13)
Surbiton High School, Kingston upon Thames

I Am . . .

I am a strawberry about to be eaten
I am the pink from the radiant flowers
I am a rabbit jumping in the wind
I am water glistening in the sea
I am a rectangle towering above other shapes
I am a sunny day putting smiles on people's faces
I dream of being able to fly.

Emma Mills (11)
Surbiton High School, Kingston upon Thames

My Studies - Shakespeare's Dream

A tragedy,
A comedy,
A love story,
A tale.
These might be the stories Shakespeare had in mind.

Sorrow,
Love,
Joy,
Fear.
These might be the feelings Shakespeare had in mind.

Famous man,
Place in history,
Theatre in London,
Stories being told.
Was this the dream Shakespeare had in mind?

Brittany Borkan (12)
Surbiton High School, Kingston upon Thames

Shakespeare's Dream

'Romeo, Romeo, where art thou Romeo.'
Witches everywhere,
Lost lovers in a deep forest.
What would you see in Shakespeare's dream?
What would you see in his mind?

Something from his plays,
Something from his life,
Something from the Globe Theatre?
Witches, fairies, princes,
Potions, confusion, betrayal.

Nightmare may occur,
Following with death and love loss,
A flash of lightning,
A red fiery glow,
The nightmares and dreams are over.

Kathryn Fletcher (12)
Surbiton High School, Kingston upon Thames

A Meeting With Shakespeare

Dewy drops trickled down the lilies' petals,
Birds chirped merrily as I skipped down the path,
Frogs leaped from lily pad to lily pad,
Disrupting the immense stillness of the water.

Bumblebees hummed loudly in my ears,
The warm breeze blew my hair wildly across my face,
The willow tree stood proudly ahead of me,
Its branches parting as if I were a king entering a room.

By the trunk there was a little silver box,
It was accompanied by a bright pink ribbon.
I grasped the mysterious object in my hands,
Then taking off the ribbon, I opened it.

Inside there was a key,
As I saw a grand looking gentleman appear over the hill,
It all became clear, I was to give the key to him,
As he came closer I saw, it was Shakespeare.

He approached me with a joyful smile,
I was told that I would be in a story,
This filled me with great excitement,
What could he want with me?

Holly Harrison (14)
Surbiton High School, Kingston upon Thames

Let's Write A Poem

I am a bouncing ball always full of energy.
I am pink like a rose about to bloom.
I am a lively dog ready to fetch.
I am a fire elegantly burning on a fire fairy.
I am a circle never-ending and full of colour.
I am a sun shining spreading happiness.
I dream of being a bubble, never able to pop.

Beth Pollington (11)
Surbiton High School, Kingston upon Thames

My Dream - In The Garden

Into the garden, the flows smell sweet,
The aroma drifts in the breeze.
Where the gravel path tapers, I spot a small box,
Catching the light under a tree.

'Oh! What is this, here on the ground,
Shining in the sun so bright?
A silver box, with something inside . . .'
I open it in excitement.

There, in the box, a golden fob watch,
A gentleman's one, not for me,
Suddenly out of the distance, a figure appears
And I know that the gift is for him.

He is of average height, not too large, not too thin
And seems to be anxious to see me.
I know this man, from my English lesson,
Of course, it's William Shakespeare!

I hand him the watch and he gives me a gift
The ability to speak his own language.
'Shakespearean English,' he calls it, quite clearly,
So I can communicate with him.

We talked and talked like we knew one another,
He told me about his new play.
He asked me to come and watch the performance,
Which I agreed to without delay.

We both had to go as the sun was setting,
While its fiery colours were glowing,
As he ran away he winked with one eye,
And disappeared into the sunset.

Viki James (13)
Surbiton High School, Kingston upon Thames

10 Bare Steps

I walked down 10 bare steps,
Towards my entrance hall,
My hand running along the smooth wooden bannister,
My eyes concentrated on the door.
I walked out into my pebbled garden,
The sun was high above my head.
It was approaching midday.
I walked down a narrow path,
The gravel crunching beneath my feet.
As I neared a large rose bush,
A small red package came into view.
Curious, I ran up to it and stooped to pick it up,
Inside was a very small carved wooden figurine,
The figurine was of a woman wearing a long flowing dress,
The expression on her face was one of amusement.
I heard footsteps and as I looked up I saw a man,
He approached slowly and as his face came into view,
I recognised him; it was Shakespeare.
He was wearing a rich red and black-striped suit,
Decorated with rich golden embroidery.
I expected him to walk past me
To my surprise he stopped just short of me
He spoke in a deep voice,
He told me that he was writing a play,
He said that he would like me to play the leading lady
He did not know who she was as he hadn't finished writing it.
I realised that the small wooden figurine was for him,
I gave it to Shakespeare and he thanked me.
Then, before I could say anything else,
He was gone - walking back up the path, away from me.
I watched him for a while, walking up the path,
Then I turned and walked back to my house,
I climbed the 10 bare steps,
Time was moving slowly now.

Atifa Jiwa (13)
Surbiton High School, Kingston upon Thames

My Golden Ring

Little red present box
Wonder what it is
It seems very special
So, I start to open it
With full of excitement
Fidgeting with my fingers

My heart beats faster and faster
Feel very nervous what is inside
Both eyeballs moving around
With my fingers
I feel very special that moment

Finally, with my deep breath
I can see very bright golden
Colour coming from little red box
Softens my eyes and covers my whole body
I knew that it was a golden ring
There as my name on it clearly
I feel more special than before

I put the golden ring back to the box
Bright golden light disappeared
Into the box with my golden ring
Then I start to walk back to the
Mirror door, reflecting the sunshine
Showing my way clearly.
I went through the door with my
Special gift which I will never forget.

Cecilia Seo (14)
Surbiton High School, Kingston upon Thames

Dream

Music begins to play
Pages fall from the sky
Book begins to drop
My head turns slightly
Lights blind me
A stage full of characters appear
Posters are passed around
'Hamlet' they say
I stand up tall
I am the star
Crowds of people fill the gaps surrounding
A blink of my eye
I am floating, gracefully in the sky
Watching myself years ago
Past memories I see
Oh I wish it were not me
My mind, so full of doom
Darkness
I lay in a bed
I rise boldly
Although I still have not awoke
A girl from years ago
Flies above watching over me
Following my every move
Oh I wish I were young
I open the door to leave when . .
Crash!
Comes from behind me
I turn to see . . .

Sophie Kiedaisch (12)
Surbiton High School, Kingston upon Thames

The Mermaid's Soul

Not so many years ago, in a town not so far from here,
A young boy and girl ran across the sands,
Into the calm sea they went to play,
The girl was never to return,
The boy called, he screamed, he shouted,
Too late, the shimmering 'Angels of the Sea' had her,
Locked up in an underwater chamber,
Her ratty hair now flowing beautifully in the waves,
She lay, still, in this peaceful world, awaiting her mermaid soul.

Rosie Morris (13)
Surbiton High School, Kingston upon Thames

The Infinite House

Floorboards whisper,
All around the building.
Long dark hallways,
That never end.
Huge dusty doors,
With infinite carvings and heavy golden handles.
Pictures old and dangling on rusty nails,
Seem as if they are in the room.
The infinite house is alive!

Amber Fraser (11)
Surbiton High School, Kingston upon Thames

I Am

I am a muffin, soft on the outside and tough inside
I am blue, a calm relaxed shade
I am a turtle expressing love through swimming
I am Earth, strong and willing
I am snow, I make people happy
I dream of a box, an infinite box,
My personality bursting and raring to be set free.

Abigail Spence (11)
Surbiton High School, Kingston upon Thames

I Am . . .

I am a baby elephant ready to take my first steps,
I am the colour of aquamarine, like pearly water,
I am an octopus, calm and mellow
I am water, because it is peaceful but also adventurous
I am a dodecahedron, because I have lots of feelings
I am a star, shining bright and high in the sky
I dream of elephants in bubbles, floating in the clouds.

Alexandra Hartley (11)
Surbiton High School, Kingston upon Thames

Mystery House

Mysterious, haunting shapes emerging from the ground.
I can hear terrifying, spine-tingling sounds mysteriously quickly.
The taste in my mouth is fear in the air.
Goosebumps are getting bigger and bigger as sharp pricks are on
the back of my neck.
I can smell rotten eggs and fish.
All the things we dread.

Laura Jones (11)
Surbiton High School, Kingston upon Thames

I Am A . . .

I am a key,
I am blue,
I am a monkey,
I am element earth,
I am circle,
I am the sun,
As I dream on and on . . .

Becky Ridpath (11)
Surbiton High School, Kingston upon Thames

Dream Vision

Dream stardust

Cherish the moment,
save the magic.

Clarity fades as it came
drifting
floating
Unreachable
like a cloud

On
a
breeze

fine as silk,
fragile as dew.
What was pin-sharp,
vivid and real as daylight,

playful
vanishes
into mist.

Chase
the dream stardust,
Catch it,
keep it,
Hold onto its precious sparkle.
Listen to its echoes
when the alarm sounds,
when the telephone rings,
sink back into that world,
treasure the memories,
pure as pearls.

Kate Hosker (15)
Surbiton High School, Kingston upon Thames

A Game Of Hide-And-Seek

There I lie, on the bottom of the seabed,
the moon is out to play; it is glistening on the top of the still,
                                        peaceful ocean,
all is quiet, as if nothing was living,
vibrant, bold colourful fish weave themselves in and out of coral - as if
                                it was a game of hide-and-seek.
I landed here from a sandy beach - you could say I had been
                                        shipwrecked,
I may have lost my friends and family,
but I certainly have not lost my dignity.
I stand up, but instead of looking down at my legs, I see a tail,
a shimmering tail; all colours of the rainbow.
The water is cold and all is still until a gush of wind sweeps me off my
                                feet - or should I say tail?
My body has become white and very frail,
I look into the misty distends of water that surrounds me,
a black gust of wind, winds itself through the ocean,
then a flash of lightning appears from the clouds.
The black hole - full of evil and betrayal, is only a couple of
                                        metres away,
the sand from the sea sure rises from the dead,
and all I can remember is when I looked ahead . . .

Molly Shingler (12)
Surbiton High School, Kingston upon Thames

A Midsummer Night's Dream

The course of true love never did run smooth.
For it twists and turns like reeds in a babbling brook.
Love is like a candle, it can be extinguished just as easily.
If love is meddled with it is hard to heal.
But lovers' quarrels are swift to heal; if mischievous Puck is involved.
Titania and Oberon madly in love, but both stubborn and sulky.
Hermia and Lysander too much in love to care for prudence.
Helena and Demetrius blind fools when it comes to love.
Bottom, an honest weaver, good but a show-off.
From dawn 'til dusk humans muddle up their lives and write
pure poetry.
But all is well at last for some, who dream a most peculiar tale of
last night's story.

'If we shadows have offended,
Think but this, and all is mended,
That you have but slumbered here
While these visions did appear'.

'Puck'.

Isabelle Bettany (11)
Surbiton High School, Kingston upon Thames

Mary-Alice Young

A girl with two brothers and two bullies,
Clever but unfortunate,
Depressed but uplifting,
Leaves school at eighteen,
Happy but sad,
Excited but nervous,
On holiday after a year,
Cornwall is a sunny place,
An old stone castle,
A witch - but
Real or fake?
A big mistake . . .

Abigail Marrow (12)
Surbiton High School, Kingston upon Thames

A Red Coral Necklace

A red coral necklace,
Shimmered on her neck,
Like little red rubies,
Against a white sandy beach.

The chain catches an eye of a magpie,
He swoops down and pecks it off,
It flies away with its new treasure,
And a tear trickles down her pure white face.

Caroline Croft (14)
Surbiton High School, Kingston upon Thames

Snap!

Canoeing in a river,
Murky and misty,
It's infested with crocodiles,
So I take extra care.
I bump into a rock,
And fall into the river.
I'm panicking and shouting,
My eyes are as big as ostrich eggs.
I see a crocodile heading for me,
Its beady eyes glare.
I try to escape,
But I'm paralysed and I can't swim.
The crocodile opens its jaws,
And before I know it,
Snap!

Amani Patel (13)
Surbiton High School, Kingston upon Thames

Journey

Ten steps was all it was,
Ten steps down my normal brown-carpeted stairs
Holding on to the bannister,
Holding it as if I was falling,
Reached the bottom,
I let go of the handrail
And took a breath,
Everything looked different,
Different wall colour,
Different carpet poking through the middle of my toes,
Where was I?
I turned left,
Into what used to be my playroom,
That too, was different.
I looked straight ahead,
The garden was different, but beautiful,
Big green trees and blackberry bushes,
Birds' singing was the only sound I heard,
Nothing else,
It felt gentle and relaxing.
As I walked down the gravel path
I saw a cylinder tied with fuchsia-pink ribbon,
The box had no label,
No address,
I untied the ribbon and opened the box,
Inside was a puppet,
A puppet of a man.
Suddenly, a hand appeared upon my shoulder,
I turned around to see a man named Shakespeare
Dressed in old-fashioned clothing,
A neck brace and a red sash,
He spoke my name,
He told me to write a play about me,
I asked him why,
He didn't reply.
I gave him the puppet which looked just like him,
He gave my cheek a kiss
As my dream went blank.

Rosie Frost (13)
Surbiton High School, Kingston upon Thames

Shakespeare's Gift

As I walked along the path,
A figure approached me,
With a manly build, it was,
One I had seen before, but
Not necessarily recognised.

The face I had seen on posters
And seen in English lessons,
With the early fashion clothes
And frills around the collar there
Was only one man that it could be.

The great writer of sonnets
And the world-known playwright was walking
Towards me, with a gift in his hand.

As we met in the pathway, I gave him a glance.
Of course, it had to be!
The one and only Shakespeare
Was standing across from me.

We engaged in conversation, and soon it became clear
He had written a play and was offering me the main part.
I was anxious at his seriousness
But accepted when he gave me
A container with a gift
As proof that he would be back.

I opened the container
And stood there in shock,
As I looked into the box.
There was a feather, with a silvery-blue stripe,
I asked what it was for,
And received a quizzical stare.

He looked at me in a very strange way
And explained that it was the main prop for the play.
I was not to lose it. As I looked back up to thank the man,
He had disappeared and was nowhere to be seen.

Ana Grgurinovic (13)
Surbiton High School, Kingston upon Thames

It's My Story

Bang!
One's gone
Another dead
Maybe the last.

They're scared
So they kill
They shoot
No mercy.

Back onshore
I find the truth
Keep it secret
Click.

I read the paper
Now it's out
I've got the money
It's my story.

They're angry
I don't know it
But one day

I will . . .

Rosie Jones (12)
Surbiton High School, Kingston upon Thames

What's The Point?

Whipped, stripped and torn away,
Beaten, broken and led astray,
My Heaven, my family and my roots,
I won't be seeing any more exotic fruits,

The mask is stuck and the bolts have jarred,
Trapped and abused by a prison guard.
I try to smile but the pain's too much,
Whilst I'm deprived from the African touch.

Rebecca Desmond & Charlotte Keenan (9)
Tolworth School for Girls, Surbiton

I Said, 'Angler'

When he fly-fishes tonight, this time he'll
aim for God, for I asked him for Heaven
in a jar, or hooked on his fishing rod,

and with my shoulders a mile below my head,
and my oesophagus in a tangle so that my heart
could not hear my words rise off the dust
I said, 'Angler, I don't much care what you catch it with,
just go back to the bank and catch me a reason to live.'

Now he looks at the stars and realises
how much closer they are,

he splays his fingers up to Heaven
and just before daybreak softly spreads a lull,
he reels down a constellation,

and slips it into my light bulb,
stealing a section from midnight
and now Orion dances upon my ceiling,
proudly marking his plight.

(Though the stars quietly protest
that it is simply stealing,
when someone like he would reel down the whole sky
for someone like me.)

Eliza Forshaw (17)
Tolworth School for Girls, Surbiton

There's No Hope

Screeching voice trembling in the closed space,
Chain manacles trembling all around this place,
We are fully frustrated - there's no hope.

Screaming and fire all around the deck,
Illness and diseases contaminating our minds,
We are fully sorrowful - there's no hope.

A moon over the sea shines brightly,
It's like she doesn't know our anguish,
Stirring desperately to the dark.

Soyoung Lee (14)
Tolworth School for Girls, Surbiton

Slavery

Our souls scream out but no one hears,
We long to leave but are trapped, no way back.
We work, work, work to the bone,
Our skin ablaze from our master's wrath.
We plead; beg, but no one cares,
We have no hope, no future, no family.
Our loved ones are gone in the blink of an eye.
Sometimes I wish I would die.

How I wish I could be with them once more,
To hear their voices, to feel their touch,
To be at home again would be as sweet as sugar,
How could I escape, be set free?
To get my revenge is my ultimate desire,
To kill them all is so cruel but seems so right,
How they can be so evil is beyond me.
I can't get to the place where I want to be.

I know I should fight, try and get away,
But I'm weak and can't go on.
Should I swim, should I fight or just think; what's the point?

What's the point?

Cara Hitt (13)
Tolworth School for Girls, Surbiton

Have I Got Dirt On My Face?

Why do they think I have dirt on my face?
I am just an ordinary person just like them.
We all have two eyes, two hands, we have the same organs,
Everything is the same, only our skin is different,
That doesn't mean that we're different.
I feel like I am an alien, am I really an alien? I ask God.
Why don't they give us a chance to tell them that we are just like them?
God, have I been put on Earth to become a slave?
God please take me to be with You.

Nadia Butt (13)
Tolworth School for Girls, Surbiton

Black Skin, Black Future

Trapped behind the bars of others,
Others of my own kind.
This isn't how it was supposed to end,
It's not just the picture I had in my mind.

Working forwards but feeling backwards,
I just can't comprehend.
Being used, but why . . . ?
Is there a reason for this new-found slavery trend?

I'm not alone this is my only comfort,
Through the darkness and the pain,
There are others like me . . .
But what does the white man gain?
Hatred?
Anything else, I doubt.

Bonita Brincat (14)
Tolworth School for Girls, Surbiton

An Animal

Gas, bombs hitting the ground.
'Quick children, put your gas masks on,' screams a helpless mum.
'Stop Edward! Don't go back!' as the boy scrambles to the house.
'No my son,' screeches Mum.' Why has my son gone back?
Bumping, pulling, he struggles back.
'My child,' the mum squeals. 'Don't you know you could have
been killed?'
He slaps his mother so hard her cheek goes red.
'No Mother, I went back for Penny . . . !'
'A dog?' the mum squeaks.
Tears running down her face, 'All for an animal,' she speaks at a pace.

Connie Noble (11)
Varndean School, Brighton

Why?

My world is hell,
Death, hatred and smell,
People kill living things,
People kill anything with wings.

Being famous is OK,
In this world, *no way!*
Why can't we all ride in TucTucs,
It's much safer for the duck ducks.

In Africa poor people dying,
The rich people always lying,
'Oh we will help them,' they say,
Will they ever? *No way!*

Maybe when the time comes,
People will realise the unfortunate ones,
Everyone is living in a hell,
The hell with the horrible smell.

Amber Pearce (11)
Varndean School, Brighton

Through The Eyes Of The Urban Eagle

Flying above the city like a spread-out map,
Above the roads and the streets and that would be that.
A game of happy families to the naked eye,
But not through the eyes of the eagle who flies high in the sky.

The clash of the cultures is a boxing match,
With religion and people fighting over fact.
When one door closes and another opens,
Maybe one is left on the latch.
The house gets burgled of good,
Truth is fired, kicked, sacked.

People are a puzzle to animals,
Driving cars plus pollution equals killing Mother Nature.

Love is the only beauty although,
It's hard to find it with all the grey covering the rainbow behind.

Through eyes of the urban eagle,
Through the eyes of many people.

Anoushka Clayton-Walshe (11)
Varndean School, Brighton

Injured

It was a fair sliding tackle,
Not one that caused the regular hassle,
In the changing room no one spoke,
Not for ages, not even on the coach.

All I could think of was the World Cup,
I couldn't be injured, anything but.
When I got to Manchester, press were all around me,
I felt sick, I just wanted my mummy.

I was in my house, watching my team,
The frustration on their faces, life is just mean.

Declan O'Reilly (11)
Varndean School, Brighton

Only The Train Station

Alone on the streets,
I see the world in a different way
The rich, the poor
The nothing.

At the age of four
I was stranded forever
So alone, so cold
Why me?

The trains are my only friends
Snooping around the busy people
No time to notice me
Snatch the food, no one sees.

The night is on its way
I hungrily head back to home
A box, in the corner
To sleep uncomfortably.

Not a wink of sleep last night
So tired, I'm practically asleep
I climb down onto the track
But when I realise, it's too late.

The horn is all I hear
But I guess that's just fate.

Megan Atkins (11)
Varndean School, Brighton

Perfect Football Debut!

P ish-posh, this can't be happening
E ven Henry didn't have a crowd this loud
R eally, this is amazing
F lying crowd
E qually flying team
C an this get any scarier and at the same time, exciting?
T his is some headline!

F ootball is great
O f course
O nly the best team has a loud crowd
T hings like this come once in a lifetime
B elieving is one thing
A ll of the people will know me afterwards
L ife is football
L ingering in the papers

D own with the other team
E ven their manager
B ut obviously in a sporting way
U nder the posts is the goalie stiff-scared
T hen we get ready and we're off!

Connor Macey (12)
Varndean School, Brighton

Untitled

Roaring tanks,
Shouting men,
The screen shrinks as a woman explains the terrors of the world.
There must be a way.

What could have been fields of crops for the hungry world,
Instead are mines and poppy fields.

Bombs erupting all around scaring people
                              with their discharging sounds.
It could have been laughter instead of screams,
It could have been the place where people have amazing dreams.

Lauren Kane-Simmons (12)
Varndean School, Brighton

A Spider's Web

The birds sing happily
The web shines for the hot sun
Glistening in the heat.

Suddenly quiet
Everything stops, frozen
Smoke rises from trees.

Quickly smoke thickens
Birds fraying animals flee
A blur, a loud cry.

Will this ever stop?
Humans destroying nature
Is this the future?

Ruby Anderson-Hawkins (11)
Varndean School, Brighton

Recipe For A Perfect Home

Begin with bags full of love
To make the home loveable.

Add a teaspoon of fun
And an ounce of games
Mix with friends
For added friendship.

Next stir in some care
In order to get fairness.

Mix it all together
And serve with a pinch of comfort.

This is a wish of a homeless person
Kicked out of their house looking for a home.

Jack Woodhouse (11)
Varndean School, Brighton

The Match

Begin with a spoonful of crowd,
This will turn the mixture cheerful and loud.
Add a pinch of grass
And a pound of stud.
This will give you a bowl of mud.

The score is 1-0,
And the ball weighs a light ml.
A packet of socks,
A jug of juice.
Then you end up with a speedy goose.

Liam Bailey (11)
Varndean School, Brighton

My Cat Life

I went outside
And jumped on a wall
I sat on the wall and I saw a slide
There was a kid on it
And he took me for a ride.

I went into the house
She had a dog
I jumped on a frog
And then the dog came
I ran and got on a climbing frame

I got outside
He was on the slide
It was him
He was a bit dim
I had a fight with him.

Jake Crunden (11)
Varndean School, Brighton

My Request

I saw a tiger
Eating a deer
I was full of fear
Because it was too near
I ran from there
I thought if I stayed there
I would not fear.

When I was trying to run away silently
I saw two bulls looking at me
I was facing the problem with fear
Do not go to the forest near.

This is my request dear!

Sujan Thapa (13)
Varndean School, Brighton

Recipe For A Perfect Football Match

Firstly begin with an acre full of grass.
Next stir in:
22 players,
A couple of packets of spectators,

Secondly, add a special edition packet of
10 subs,
2 managers,
1 coach,
1 4th official
2 linesmen and a referee.

Thirdly, add a couple thousand bricks,
A few drops of cement and stir until light and fluffy.
Put everything together and stir until ready.

Finally put in the oven for 90 minutes,
And halfway through take out for 15 minutes
And *enjoy!*

Alex Bradley (11)
Varndean School, Brighton

The Recipe For A Perfect Dart Player

First take a bucket of luck,
Stir in lots of skill.
Next take three sharp shiny points,
Add long sleek stems.
Then roll around in your hands until nice and warm,
Add a spoonful of stem grips.
Take a cupful of bull's-eyes, mix all together.
For a finishing touch, add a sprinkle of flights.
Then serve with a nice chilled pint of orange juice and lemonade.
That's how you get the perfect dart player . . .
                    My dad!

Eleanor Sopp (11)
Varndean School, Brighton

Tiger Eyes And Tiger Thoughts

I wake up to the sound of screams,
With angry roars mixed in,
Three booming shots ring out,
And the chainsaws keep ringing.

I've been wandering for days,
I've shrunk to a pile of skin and bones,
My home is a pile of sticks and mud,
And the chainsaws keep ringing.

I'm scared and weak,
All the food is gone,
I'm starving to my lonely death,
And the chainsaws keep ringing.

I'm limp and frail,
Death has greeted me,
I'm glad to leave this cruel cold world,
And the chainsaws keep ringing.

A penny for your thoughts!

Tallulah Pepperell (11)
Varndean School, Brighton

My Life On The Streets

It all started when I looked at the flat
Mum chucked my clothes out
And then I met Matt, he gave me a place on my first night
He said it was a delight.

I now wander around with no place to go
But Mum's is a big *no!*
I see Matt from time to time
He's just been put down for a crime.

I get back at nine
To where I've been squatting for some time
But I guess it's all mine.

Jack Lawrence (11)
Varndean School, Brighton

The System

There's no John F Kennedy or Woody Guthrie
And reality has become TV.

Everything has ended, but nothing has begun.

They call it 'the system', and it controls everyone.

I'm gonna talk about my generation
God, I hope they can clean up this nation
I know we're lucky, we shouldn't take things for granted,
But things could get worse, God forbid!

Someone, anyone, must do something.

They call it 'the system', and it controls everything.

I don't expect planet Earth to be Heaven
But the world is nearly over in 2007!

Ned Wall (12)
Varndean School, Brighton

I'm Only A Baby

The morning hustle,
The bustle,
The rustle of Mum wrapping a sandwich for Grace's lunch.

Dad's stuffing food into my mouth . . .
Oops! I coughed
All over Dad's new shirt,
Oh God, he's gonna kill me!

Mum's running late,
Dad's running late,
Grace is picking at the cake Mum's just baked.

Why is it all so crazy?
I'm only a baby.
They should all just slow down,
Take a minute to relax, kick back!

Matt Morrish (11)
Varndean School, Brighton

The Beast Is Prowling

I'm in the forest hunting
I'm in the forest now
I'm in the forest with the beast on the prowl.

I can hear the beast moaning
I can hear the beast groaning
But now all I can hear is nothing . . .

Now I can hear something
Now I can smell something
Now I can see the beast on the prowl.

He's coming at me fast
He's coming at me steady
He's coming at me now
I'd better be ready . . .

Navan Jarnail Singh Johal (11)
Varndean School, Brighton

Your World - The Brain

Unlock the world
If you believe you can achieve
Don't get frustrated, you can do it
Think of the world as a brain
Part of the world is you
So don't let the world down
You can make a change
Who knows what the meaning is
Does it really matter?
Just try
You can do it
Some people are strong, some are weak
Your heart is the door
Now find the key
Let out your thoughts!

Olivia Sewell (11)
Varndean School, Brighton

The Chase Of The Tiger And The Mouse

I'm the mighty tiger bold and brave,
My stripes will make you hide in a cave.

I make the trees shake,
I cause an earthquake.
What's that I see?
A mouse hanging off a tree!

I'm creeping slowly towards the mouse,
Hey wait a minute, I see a house!
Oh no the mouse has run away,
I'd better find him before the end of day!

So I go towards the house,
To try and find the mouse,
I think I see him behind the door,
Me and this mouse shall have a war!

Raya Alkhayal (11) & Alyce Orford (12)
Varndean School, Brighton

Life As A Seagull

My children are starving,
I need more help,
I need to make sure they're not upset.

I search the bins for more food,
I don't know what to do,
Life as a seagull is hard for me and you.

I fly across the shiny sea,
For my special babies,
They need to live for more generations,
But I hope they will have more food than me.

Louise Flowers (11)
Varndean School, Brighton

Little Bird

I see a bird up in the sky,
I look out of my window and say, 'Oh my!'
It's black and brown and spins around on the grass in the dirty ground.
But then the bird is trapped by Mr Whiskers, the neighbour's cat,
I can see the bird in total fright,
But then it flies off out of my sight.
Fly little bird, fly, fly, fly,
For tomorrow will be another day in the deep blue sky.

Jordan Crunden (11)
Varndean School, Brighton

Recipe For My Favourite Football Match!

Start with bags full of goals to make it entertaining
Add a dash of scoring opportunities
To make you pull your hair out.

Stir in a pinch of saves to make it dramatic
Mix in a teaspoon of free kicks to ease the tension
Serve with a Manchester United win
To make the crowd *cheer!*

Ian Penny (11)
Varndean School, Brighton

Through The Eyes Of A . . .

D oe-eyed diver of the
O ceans, laughing
L oving, leaping
P eerless performer
H appy hunter
I nquisitive
N avigator of the sea.

Ciara Smith (11)
Varndean School, Brighton

Say Stop!

I was sitting on the bus,
When I heard quite a fuss.

A teen with piercings, those were small,
And an old lady with none at all.

'I'm not gonna get up for you,' the teenager said.
The old lady replied, 'You obviously got up on the wrong side
of the bed.'

'In my day,' she told the teen who wasn't listening,
'We listened to what our elders were saying.

We did not have fancy cars or rings,
And we certainly did not say words like 'fing'.

In fact we had hardly anything,
And in my day we made our own living.

At least we knew how to be polite,
You lot are just as disgusting as Marmite.'

'What's wrong with saying 'fing' anyway?
And you are not getting my seat,' I heard the teen say.

'You know in my day,' the old lady started to say as if she had
been cursed.
The teenager said, 'Yeah well times change and I was here first.'

Then before I knew it the lady was pushed onto the floor,
And the teen was asked to leave the bus as he pushed past to get to
the door.

So is this what we want the future to be full of?
Crime and abuse is all we can see ahead of us.

I wish I could have done something and not been such a mop.
So next time don't just sit and watch, say *stop*.

Shona Kumar (13)
Wallington High School for Girls, Wallington

What You Really Mean

Sheer embarrassment
When your mum kisses you goodbye.
You say get off,
You mean goodbye.

Sheer embarrassment
When your mum tells you that there's dirt on your face.
You say whatever,
You mean where.

Sheer embarrassment
When your mum picks you up halfway through a party
Announcing to your friends it's your bedtime.
You say go away,
You mean please let me stay.

Sheer embarrassment
When your mum says she loves you.
You say nothing,
You mean I love you too.

But behind all that embarrassment,
Behind your straight face,
Deep down in your heart,
You have much more to say.

If people spoke from their heart,
Instead of their brain,
The world would be so much louder again.

Hannah Oram (13)
Wallington High School for Girls, Wallington

When I Look Into The Future

When I look into the future this is what I see
A cure for cancer, a substitute for coal
Heroes, this is what we'll be

When I look into the future this is what I see
A river with no pollution, junk or mess
Just the little fish and me

When I look into the future this is what I see
A high school chum and a qualified nurse
Placing a bandage on a knee

When I look into the future this is what I see
A flock of hover cars, and huge jet-packs
Flying elegantly and free

When I look into the future this is what I see
A cure for cancer, a substitute for coal
Heroes, this is what we'll be.

Shaili Desai (13)
Wallington High School for Girls, Wallington

Mobile Phones - Yesterday, Today And Tomorrow

Yesterday was a communication brick,
AKA a mobile that is thick,
Today there's an mp3, camera, flip phone,
Folk may say a flashy dog and bone,
Tomorrow there'll be a phone that speaks for you,
Or one that's smaller than a corkscrew.
We have no idea what'll be next,
Why not a simple phone that can text?
This mobile craze is so overrated,
Should not be so exaggerated.
So we don't know what'll be next to happen,
But I'm sure the price range will widen.

Xanthe Francis (12)
Wallington High School for Girls, Wallington

The Truth

This is about us, how we feel,
A chance to say and speak the truth.
People think bad thoughts about us youths.
We are constantly misunderstood.
Trying to say something but never heard.
Makes us feel the only way we can be seen,
Is by committing crimes, upsetting our society.
Disrespectful and lazy are common names we are called,
But they don't care whether it hurts us or not.
We want to be the best people we can,
But when we try, we keep getting pulled down.
If they give us some courage, support and respect,
Maybe we'll be happy and be ourselves again.
We are disguised as people we're not.
If we work together, together, we can take our masks off.

Thayaruby Uthayakumaranathan (12)
Wallington High School for Girls, Wallington

My Life As A Chair

In the old times, I lived with two old people, they were a lovely couple,
But they had to sell me as they became very poor.
Now I lived with this ungrateful family,
Children jump on me!
Children rocking on me!
Hopping on to me as if I'm something without a life!
I feel so old as if I'm going to collapse any time.
Any day . . . at any time . . . at any minute . . .
I'm going to d . . .

Poongkayl Birabaharan (12)
Wallington High School for Girls, Wallington

Talkin' 'Bout My Generation

Through the eyes of a whole different world, a different country,
There is a different scene to see.
Humid and hot surroundings don't help their pains,
Of everyday life and all of its strains.
Make-up and looks and clothes and 'high tech'
Soon becomes the responsibilities of our lives.

We don't know the condition or reality
Of their real life and what they do daily.
Water, food and family are their essentials,
Their education and work doesn't show much potential,
Tell me why they are like this,
Tell me why we live like this.

Our age, our look, our personality,
But we live in England, they live in poverty.
We have money, a home and a chance,
To help out and to thoughtfully grant
But we get sucked into a land of media and fun,
No bother or time taken for the ones left behind.

Jenny Fox (13)
Wallington High School for Girls, Wallington

Labelled

We're split into categories,
Labelled and named.
But what is the point?
No one's the same.

So what, I like rap music,
It doesn't make me a chav.
And if I wear dark glasses,
Emo, that's the label I'll have.

All of us are different,
Not one of us the same.
So tell me why people do this,
Give us all another name.

When will you realise that I'm just me,
I'm an individual, the only one left,
So when you give me a label,
I think *unique* would be best.

Megan Hughes (14)
Wallington High School for Girls, Wallington

From Furbys To Tamagotchis

I was born in mid nineties,
Things were really old.
We were fascinated by Tamagotchis
And I had a troll doll.

As we got older, time moved on,
Furbys were no longer fun,
Then *bang,* we hit the new millennium,
Nothing was the same again.

PlayStation 1s became a trend,
As well as Bayblades and Pokémon.
Harry Potter became cool,
Our new generation had just begun.

Soon after, in secondary school,
Where I am right now,
Things had changed enormously,
And I will tell you how.

Ipods soon took over,
IKEA is the best,
Internet is quicker,
And we all read less.

I like both parts of my generation,
Simply just as,
It is how I grew up,
And I would never ask for more.

Serina Kitazono (13)
Wallington High School for Girls, Wallington

My Generation

If I could look back at the past
Sitting reminiscing about the good days,
Nothing was as bad as it used to be,
The streets were safe,
Everyone you met was safe,
Why can't it be like that now?

But nowadays everyone's ashamed of the youth
Cos the truth looks strange,
And for me it's a first, it shouldn't be like this
And it hurts.

Guns triggers pressed,
Knives stabbed, we're all depressed.
We're so far from the way it should be,
Hard workers, fast workers, that's how it should be,
Why couldn't it be like that now?

Being a nerd, neek or a geek
Makes you strong, not a freak.
Don't be afraid, don't be ashamed
Of whom you are,
Forget the rest.

If this is life for our next generation,
Am I proud? Far from it.
Working together,
Together as a team
We can bring back the way it should be.

Zainab Haq (13)
Wallington High School for Girls, Wallington

Talkin' 'Bout My Generation

It's Monday morning and I'm off to collect my pension,
There are yobs on the bus, too many to mention.
They're a menace to society, the youth of today,
All they care about is getting a lay.

The young ones outside the post office agitate me,
I'm oh so nervous, I just want some tea.
They don't look like they've even seen a cuppa,
They're just too busy trying to mug ya.

They start looking my way and stare,
I don't know what to do so I give them a glare.
Disgusting layabouts, it's not like they have feelings,
With all their dodgy wheelings and dealings.

They swear and start to come over,
I run away, looking over my shoulder.
They are coming at me, all scary and fat,
In my dismay I trip over a cat.

It was really lucky I didn't fall on my face,
It's just a shame I wasn't carrying my mace.
I lay on the road on my back,
Everything swirls then suddenly goes black.

I wake up all alone in a hospital ward,
My head feeling like it's been attacked with a sword.
I sat up and found the group of kids standing there,
But now, they didn't even give me a scare.

One of them had grapes for me in a little basket,
And they're the reason I'm not in a casket.
I guess I'd misjudged his balaclava and hood,
I guess underneath it all, they're only misunderstood.

Joanne Brogan (13)
Wallington High School for Girls, Wallington

It's A Girl's Life

Confused feelings
Lots of laughs
Nasty girls
These are in a girl's life.

Time with mates
Schoolwork
Moaning parents
These are a girl's life.

Stupid boys
Make-up tips
Glossy magazines
These are in a girl's life.

Hair straighteners
Skinny jeans
Glitter heels
These are in a girl's life.

Late night phone calls
Important parties
Mobile phones
These are in a girl's life.

Taking risks
Private doodles
Peer pressure
These are in a girl's life.

It's really not as easy as it sounds
But we put on a fake smile
To help us through the ups and downs
Of living a girl's life.

Phoebe Gomes (13)
Wallington High School for Girls, Wallington

Why Can't You Understand?

It is Monday again, gotta get up extra early,
Need to get my younger sisters ready for school,
Got detention cos my sister chewed up my book,
Couldn't pick up my sisters so my mum shouted.

My alarm broke so I got up late,
Late for school and left sisters at home,
Tried to make dinner but ran out of food,
All alone as Mum's not home.

Got my sisters ready for school,
Missed the bus and had to walk,
Home from school; Mum is back,
She went to the pub but didn't tell.

Didn't get up cos can't face school,
Mum told me to clean the kitchen,
Police gave me a caution for truancy,
Mum told me off; why doesn't she understand?

Got up early and woke Mum up,
She said to leave her alone,
Wanted to do homework,
But I had to babysit the kids.

Got up early to do homework,
Mum sent me to the supermarket,
I cooked dinner when Mum went out,
Still haven't done my homework.

Gonna get detention,
As I haven't done my homework,
Kids are hyper and I can't calm them down,
The end of the week and it will all start again,
Why doesn't anyone understand?

Aisha Nottage (13)
Wallington High School for Girls, Wallington

Question Mark

How can I know?
There's way too much to choose from.
Walk or the bus?
Either way doesn't take long.
Should I own up?
But I don't wanna be in trouble.

Burger or salad?
But I really deserve a treat.
Go to bed or watch TV?
I missed the last episode.
Live with Mum or Dad?
I really love them both.

The choice is just too much,
How can this be?
Do history or geography for GCSE?
I'm rubbish at both.
Revise for the test now?
I'll just do it tomorrow.

Stand up for elders on the bus?
They're as able as me to stand,
They've got less time to live.

I can't make up my mind,
This isn't right,
Life really, really is not kind.

Oyinda Ayonrinde (13)
Wallington High School for Girls, Wallington

Destroying Our World

The 21st century is very bad,
There are many people who are quite mad,
They drink and drive and destroy other lives,
Or murder children with some knives.
Every day the news is tragic,
More people dead as if by magic,
But where are the police? They're meant to be good,
They're meant to be saving lives if they could.
Every day the world gets worse,
As if we all have some kind of curse.
Where is God? He's meant to be here,
But after all, why would He care?
We are destroying our world, but what does it matter?
We stuff our faces and become a lot fatter.
The government's changed and now it's all new,
The rubbish is worse and the recycling too.
Taxes rise and pay cheques don't lower,
The government policies become a lot slower.
Global warming is becoming very bad,
The world has changed and it makes me sad.

Camilla Prowse (14)
Wallington High School for Girls, Wallington

Internet Life

I'm typing all day long
Fixed upon this screen
I walk into the chat room
And see who's feeling keen

The minutes fly past fast
My eyes are turning square
Comment for comment, code for code
Don't buy music, we share

It's really quite a sad life
Online friends all the way
Lack of social contact
Is what they always say

Though you can be who you want
No one judges you on looks
Cos everything's a lie
Until you start to hook

That's when the problems start
When it all goes so bad
I've been gone for weeks
Because I was chatroom mad.

Sabina Wantoch (13)
Wallington High School for Girls, Wallington

Love Unseen

I love the way you talk, I love the way you stand,
I love the way you do your thing, but I wish you'd take my hand.
I haven't said I love you, but I really do,
I'd be glad and so not sad if it were me and you.
I stare at you from my window, wishing you could see
How great it would be for both of us, if it were you and me.
But you never seem to look, you never seem to care,
You ignore the girl inside who is waiting for you there.
I'm not heard, not seen by you, just the invisible girl
From across the world, who feels a need for you.
Whenever I look, you turn away, I feel as if I'll fade away,
I wish you'd take a second look,
Not leave me hanging on the hook.
I feel so alone, lost in a world of broken dreams,
My heart is as cold as ice, stuck in a void of heartfelt schemes.
My body feels empty, hollow as a shoe,
Just a transparent girl in a lonely world, with no one to love but you.
How you rip and tear my heart, you ignored me from the start,
But I love you through and through, I'll always be there for you.

Jessica Quinney (13)
Wallington High School for Girls, Wallington

School Day Rap

I wake up in the late afternoon,
I'll call Sarah just to she how she's doin',
It goes straight to voicemail,
I'll send her a text, she replies without fail.
We're chattin' for ages on our mobile phones,
I tell her all about my brand new ringtone,
I look at my watch and shout OMG!
I'm late for school, it's quarter past three.
I grab my bag and run for the bus,
I think school is way too much fuss.
I show my Oyster card to the driver,
Then I sit down with my mp3 player.
I look up to see a guy named Paul,
He's lookin' at me like I'm disrespectful.
I jump off the bus outside my school,
My shirt's tucked in, I look such a fool.
I'm off to science on the second floor,
I'll have loads of homework, that's for sure.
Old people think that they're all that,
But it's the youth of today where it's at.

Florrie Sheehan (13)
Wallington High School for Girls, Wallington

Bullied Because I Care

B ecause I care about the environment,
U sually I am teased,
L ately my mind has been far from eased.
L ook at the world around you,
I t's being destroyed,
E nergy is being created in the wrong way,
D on't tease me

B ecause of my worries,
E nd it now
C ould you please?
A nnoyed is me because of you and the world,
U nder threat are our grandchildren,
S illy it seems until you really think about it.
E njoy the world we are living in today.

I n cars we travel not at their full capacity,

C ould we stick to tenacity
A nd maybe succeed in making the world a better place for the
                                        future generations?
R est your case and help me save the world.
E njoy it and please *don't bully me because I care!*

Jennifer Marie Gorvin (14)
Wallington High School for Girls, Wallington

School Day

Wake up so early and do my hair,
Put on my make-up because I don't care,
Don't eat any breakfast I'm late already,
Walk to school with my bag that's so heavy,
Stand outside by the bus stop,
Talk to the guys till they rush off,
Go inside to my form room,
Get my books out and I'm ready for doom,
Four hours later and I'm really hungry,
Get to the canteen in a hurry,
Push to the front and get some food,
All the canteen ladies are in a bad mood,
Eat and chat to everyone,
Lunch is always so much fun,
Just one more lesson to go,
It will be so boring in maths, oh no,
Go to the toilets and put more make-up on,
We're gonna miss the bus, better run,
Caught it just in time,
So now is lazy time!

Stevie Gibbs (14)
Wallington High School for Girls, Wallington

All Alone

Any minute now
They'll be looking for me
Any minute now
I'll be long gone
Any minute now
I'll be all on my own,
Away from this world, long gone
Young and free, open to the world
No school, no work
No one to tell me what to do
No one to say no
Or tell me where to go
But still far from home
All alone
The wind blowing in my hair
The natural flavour of life
I reach the beach
The sand blowing blissfully
And I think and think
Of what lays for me back at home
The stress, the pain
Of a broken family, what more am I to do
Abused and used, no one left to care for
I see the ocean sparkly and blue
And I think, wouldn't it be nice?
So I jump and I go under
But what now?
I should have stayed strong and made a difference.
All alone.

Romina Fallah (13)
Wallington High School for Girls, Wallington

Changes

These days the technology is very advanced
Computers, TVs imported from France
Another one of this addiction
Is the PlayStation 2 filled with fiction
The world's a modern place

Crimes seem to be taking over
Making the lost one's families sober
Knives, fists, stabbing and guns
Seem to be the teenager's idea of fun
The world's a dangerous place

Girls indeed like to dress to impress
Whether you like to look like a chav or a princess
They own skirts, shoes, jeans, tops and bags
But you will never find any rags
The world's a fashionable place

Peer pressure a common thing
Bulimia, drugs, smoking and dieting
A reputation they feel they have to keep
The consequences will make them weep
The world's a sad place

Education is a must
For students it's a thrust
Science an exciting subject
Inventions made to make the perfect object
The world's a creative place.

Ishani Phakkey (13)
Wallington High School for Girls, Wallington

A Baby And Her Big Sis

Yawn, nice long nap in a summer's afternoon,
Big sis picks me up and pats me on the back,
Burp. That's a relief,
She's on the phone to a guy called Jack.

She speaks in a weird language,
Innit, whatever, yeah man,
But what does it mean?
The only words I ever hear are yes, no and aren't you so cute!

Her cap is on to the side,
Her skirt is shorter than my nappy,
Her eyes are black and her eyelashes long,
And, wow, is she so chatty!

She sits herself on the couch,
And puts me in her lap,
But boy I wish I wasn't here,
I think my eardrums are popping!

I feel confused as to why she is different,
She always goes out at night,
And comes back way after I'm asleep,
And sometimes when it's turning light.

I hear Dad saying, 'She's just a teenager,'
So is that me in 14 years time?
I hope not because Sis always seems angry,
And hardly ever spends time with me.

Yes, I'm back with Mum,
Finally, I can hear Ts being said,
I wonder if I'll become like Sis when I'm older,
Or will things have changed for the better?

Delphine Appadurai (13)
Wallington High School for Girls, Wallington

Butterfly

If I were a butterfly
And had nothing else to do,
I think I would just flutter by
And take a look at you.

You used to be a bundle
Of small thoughts and delight,
And gaze at me in wonder
As I swooped in flight.

When you grew to five years old
You caught me in a net,
You were so very clever,
No one else has caught me yet.

But then you grew to nine and ten
And the changes began to start.
You tried to burn me in a glass
And nearly broke my heart.

Soon you spent the sunny days
Staring at a screen,
You seemed to want everyone
To think of you as mean.

As the years dragged on and on
You changed a whole lot more,
You answered back, you hit, you punched,
You drank, you smoked, you swore.
You were quite, quite different from the boy you were before.

And as you pave the streets tonight,
Looking out to start a fight,
I wonder as I flutter by
If you remember me, your butterfly.

Catherine Brett (13)
Wallington High School for Girls, Wallington

A War In May

I could see blood everywhere
And a lot of people dying there
Still the soldiers were shooting
While some people were shouting

Everyone was on the moor
And even some on the floor
Not knowing what to say
In the sorrow month of May

Lots of blood was on the ground
And Peter had a very big wound
Then came the strong rain
To give us even more pain

No one had the power to run
There was nothing to eat, not even a bun
But luckily, water was seen
It was miles away, probably fifteen

All of us were dying of hunger
And our bodies were filled with anger
I really wanted to run away
But the evil soldiers made me stay

They were glaring with evil eyes
And then came the little flies
Dead bodies were now rotting
Which left the poor people crying.

Meneka Kanagaratnam (14)
Wallington High School for Girls, Wallington

The Adults Got It Wrong . . . Again!

So misunderstood,
So many lies,
So full of talk,
They don't hear the cries.

They don't understand,
What we feel inside,
They don't really care,
What we try to hide.

We don't have a chance,
To prove them wrong,
It just comes to them,
As a pitiful song.

They do not care,
About our feelings so deep,
They do not know,
That I cannot sleep.

Why is it
That I'm never right?
I'm not strong enough,
To always win the fight.

Adults think they are so amazing,
They think they rule the world,
Yet it's the rules they made,
That they have curled.

Lia Burnell (13)
Wallington High School for Girls, Wallington

Then And Now

Today is very different
To 50 years ago
Crime has become a way of life
I want you all to know

Safety is an issue
That has completely changed
Guns and knives are everywhere
Control needs to be regained

Kids as young as 10 years old
Carry knives and guns
They use them and destroy their life
And end up on the run

Gangs and thugs hang around
On corners everywhere
Shouting, screaming, swearing
It's more than some can bear

We need to sort the problem out
Get rid of guns and crime
We need to sort it out right *now*
While we still have the time.

Rachael Maudsley (14)
Wallington High School for Girls, Wallington

Around Again

Early morning on an autumn day
I see the leaves
Blowing away
Colours of brown, orange and red
Falling down
And making a bed

The cold sets in
It's dark and dim
The trees look bare
And winter's here

Around the corner
And it is spring
Flowers bloom
And birds begin to sing

It's summertime
The sun is out
Under the tree
I sit and wait

I see a leaf
Fall on me
Is it autumn
Around again?

Caroline D'Mello (13)
Wallington High School for Girls, Wallington

Teenage Imagination

There's a place in my imagination
Of a perfect world next door
And our parents say we can go there
If we don't hate anymore
But they don't understand
That we don't forgive that fast
'Cause when we are teenagers
Our memories are built to last

Our imaginations all hold a place
We think is the perfect world
Without parents telling us we've been bad
When we don't do what we're told
But sometimes, it's nice to be told what to do
When you're unsure of where to turn
And maybe if we listened once in a while
We'd have something new to learn

When you want to go out to hang with your friends
And your parents say it's too late
When you want to eat sweets and take-outs all the time
But they want you to eat off a plate
These are all things we find so annoying
Them telling us what to do
But if we grow old and fat on the sofa
We'll be glad for it too.

Harriet Evans (13)
Wallington High School for Girls, Wallington

It's A Teen Thing

At the start of the year, teens worldwide
Are fresh and attentive, ready for the ride.
They make resolutions and promise to keep them,
To work harder at school, make diets and stick with them.
But a week back at school and we're falling asleep,
At home, on the bus, in lessons, all week.
There is homework, friends and parties in the park
That keep us from home from dawn till it's dark.
We are the techno generation, so TVs are needed too,
As well as computers, CD players and iPods, brand new.
We are growing up with the world pressing us down,
Global warming and pollution can make anyone frown.
Never mind - some day we're gonna find the solution
To freeze back the ice caps and clean out all pollution!
So long as we're allowed to go on MSN,
We'll fix the world, clean it up, there and then.
Though shouting and wrongdoing is what we do best,
We can smile and work hard when put to the test.
Let's face it - we can work the TV and DVD players too
Which is sometimes much more than most adults can do!
Even when we are old, we'll be glued to the PlayStation
Because we are the kids of today's generation.

Rhiannon Roy (13)
Wallington High School for Girls, Wallington

Do You Mind?

When I see gangs on the street I'll cross over
I don't mind
When they stare, I'll stare back or look away
I don't mind
When they walk past and ignore me
I don't mind
When they act cool for their friends
I don't mind
When they sit by the bus stops, I'll walk
I don't mind
But what I do mind is what people think of our generation
I mind, but do you?

If we hang in gangs we're being troublemakers or yobs
I mind
If we ignore people we're being antisocial
I mind
If we wear hoodies people think we've got knives
I mind
If we chat to friends we're talking a different language
I mind
If we don't look at people in the street we're disrespectful
I mind.

Adults think we're worth ASBOs and should be locked up
I mind
Adults say things have changed since their time when they haven't
I mind
Adults think a lot of things, but they know nothing of our generation
I mind, but do you?

Jenny Munden (13)
Wallington High School for Girls, Wallington

Can You Guess Who Am I?

Oops, I've woken up the family
Downstairs they've all come
They're all having breakfast
Oh, now I'm having some.

Dad's got the toys
We're off to the park!
I can see my other friends
Who was it that just barked?

Mum's off to school
With the boys in tow
Dad and the girls
Really have to go.

Mum's still at the shops
My toys are getting boring
I hope she buys me some
Here she comes, with the shopping.

Ah, how exhausted I am
We've just gone for a walk
Now I can hear the telephone
Mum's set for a long, long talk.

Gina's home from school
She's on her iPod now
Oblivious to anything else
She won't play with me, ow!

Oops, got in the way of the Hoover
It's sooo loud
I do love this family
And to be part of it I'm proud.

Amy O'Connor (13)
Wallington High School for Girls, Wallington

Me And The Streets

'Tis my home now, 'ere on the streets,
All I can do is listen to the teens with their new beats.
I hate how the people stare and point,
They probably think I'm here because I'm on the joint.
I sit and wait here all day,
Just letting my life drain away.
Having no one to talk to is the worst,
I feel I have been cursed.
Why am I here?
And why do all the people have to sneer?
I watch the cars go by,
While I lie here in this tunnel.
The dirt covers me, dust in my eyes.
It is now night;
This is when I am scared the most.
Thinking that this may be my last,
Then a group of chavs come past,
Calling me mean words, shouting, laughing at me,
They start kicking, punching, why can't they see?
I don't want to be here, all on my own.
Tomorrow is a fresh start.
I cannot stay on the streets any longer;
No, I will not . . .

Alexandra Vaal (14)
Wallington High School for Girls, Wallington

Analogous Worlds

Whilst England's young teens roam the streets,
Worrying about what to wear tomorrow,
Young African children across the world,
Grieve over lost loved ones weeping in sorrow.

As the diverse groups of England conflict with other kinds,
Over dress styles, slang lingo and things that differentiate each other,
Orphan kids in paralleling countries,
Wish on the life of their mother.

Just as we find faults in our lives,
Or complain we do not have enough cash,
Starving infants' hopes are fading,
When they can't find food scraps in trash.

How normal it is for us to desire an mp4,
Or the newest, flattest screened TV,
But teens in Gambia also have dreams,
That a doctor will come or even a health facility.

While we search for our ringing, flash mobiles,
Or our missing pencil case,
Chinese parents ransack for their kidnapped child,
Or forage for a dry sleeping place.

Young people just like me, in our generation,
Have such different distinguishable paths,
Our worlds are so comparable and unlike,
When both live on the same Earth and time, how are lives so contrast?

Georgina Bellman (14)
Wallington High School for Girls, Wallington

Changing Styles

100 years ago,
The things the kids did wear
Were dresses and smart suits,
They did not really care.

Now it has all changed,
There are many different styles.
To get the latest looks,
People go for miles.

Some wear tracksuit bottoms,
And big hoodies as well.
Others just wear jeans
As they take so long to dwell.

A few people wear caps
And more have little bags.
Some have cute hair bands,
Or designer tags.

More have comfy trainers,
Others wear fashionable Crocs.
A few have little pumps,
People think their shoes rock.

So style has developed,
A very long way.
Youths wear different stuff,
Every single day.

Laura Rogers (13)
Wallington High School for Girls, Wallington

Ouija

Exorcise your misery
Turn into poetry
Sheer celluloid alchemy
Upturned inkpot becomes flesh

Write, I begged you, write and live
So I can read you, own and devour
Succulent dark substance of your mind
Gorged, I will lay with your reflections
Distorted, nebulous and narcissistic
Orthography Drowning
The Madness of King Grammar

Haunted you were, haunting
     That tabloid charnel-house of a library
       Bloated with celebrity biographies
         Teen fiction, furies, flies, atrocities
           You stacked them diligently, alphabetically:
Angst burns, contrives desires, even the October foliage growls, howls
in juxtaposition, kaleidoscopically lunges at me, non compos mentis –

           I distracted you. My mouth
           Was a cataract frothing vile and lustful
           Poetry, Medusan hair and manic
           Eyes pleading accusingly
           Why don't you write? I want you, wantonly
           Uncork the dulcet venoms of your heart!
           Squeeze out the marrow of your ivory bones!

           But bloodless you were, guiding
        Me tactfully towards my Shakespeare
      Thumbed my thousands, loved by few
    Then you continued, silent undertaker
Wistfully amid the rows.

Myroslava Halushka (17)
Wallington High School for Girls, Wallington

Young Writers Information

We hope you have enjoyed reading this book - and that you will continue to enjoy it in the coming years.

If you like reading and writing poetry drop us a line, or give us a call, and we'll send you a free information pack.

Alternatively if you would like to order further copies of this book or any of our other titles, then please give us a call or log onto our website at www.youngwriters.co.uk

Young Writers Information
Remus House
Coltsfoot Drive
Peterborough
PE2 9JX

(01733) 890066